REDEFINE SUCCESS *for* WOMEN

REDEFINE SUCCESS *for* WOMEN

A PROVEN BLUEPRINT TO DESIGN A FULFILLING LIFE

JANUARY DONOVAN

THE WOMAN SCHOOL FOUNDER

Redefine Success For Women, A Proven Blueprint to Design a Fulfilling Life © 2022 by January Donovan. All rights reserved. No part of this book may be reproduced by any mechanical, photographic, or electronic process, or in the form of a phonographic recording; nor may it be stored in a retrieval system, transmitted, or otherwise be copied for public or private use—other than for "fair use" as brief quotations embodied in articles and reviews—without prior written permission of The Woman School and/or its members. The author of this workbook offers information of a general nature to help you in your quest for wholeness. This workbook is not designed to be a definitive guide or to take the place of advice from a qualified professional, and there is no guarantee that the methods suggested in this workbook will be successful. Thus, neither the publisher nor the author assumes liability for any losses that may be sustained by the use of the methods described in this workbook, and any such liability is hereby expressly disclaimed. In the event you use any of the information in this workbook for yourself, the Woman School and/or its members assume no responsibility for your actions.

THE W✸MAN SCHOOL

6070 National Blvd, Unit 223, Ave Maria, FL 34142

Edited by Mary Delgado

Send feedback to admin@thewomanschool.com

thewomanschool.com | redefinesuccessforwomen.com

ISBN: 979-8-9875236-0-5 - paperback
ISBN: 979-8-9875236-1-2 - hardcover
ISBN: 979-8-9875236-2-9 - ebook

REDEFINE SUCCESS FOR WOMEN

"LET US DARE TO CHANGE THE WORLD BEGINNING WITH OUR INTERIOR WORLD."

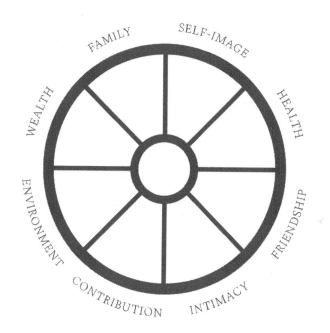

JANUARY DONOVAN - FOUNDER
THE W✹MAN SCHOOL

LEARN MORE ABOUT OUR SCHOOLS

WWW.THEWHOLENESSSCHOOL.COM

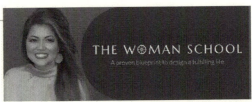

THEWOMANSCHOOL.COM

THEWHOLENESSSCHOOL.COM

THEWHOLENESSCOACHINGSCHOOL.COM

THEWHOLENESSSCHOOL.COM

ABOUT JANUARY DONOVAN

January Donovan is the founder of The Woman School and The Wholeness Coaching School. She is a #1 best-selling author, entrepreneur, and mother of eight children. She has over twenty years of experience in training women into a life of wholeness.

January had a bold dream to build a school that would offer women mindset and skill set training to help them design a fulfilling life. She spent over fifteen years training women for free before realizing that in order to reach millions, she had to learn to build a business while prioritizing her family.

The business grew into a multimillion-dollar company reaching thousands of students across forty countries in under three years and landed her the title of one of Forbes Magazine's Top Coaches.

She went on to cofound The Wholeness Coaching School with her husband Ryan, where she teaches men and women to build their own coaching businesses using mindset and skill set training to help people design a life of wholeness. Together, they also founded The Man School and quickly expanded to The Woman School en Español.

January's dream fuels her discipline as a wife, mother, and business owner because we can't give what we do not have. We were created to live a life of meaning and contribution, we just need to *train-up* for it.

January believes that life without skills is hard, and skills give us choices. We suffer unnecessary overwhelm, stress, and anxiety simply because we are undertrained. We battle feeling like a failure when in reality, the world has failed to prepare us. We can no longer afford to hand over a generation of men and women who doubt their worth and give up on who they were created to be because they lack the skills. Training and discipline are essential to achieving the life that we want.

She believes that it is time to recognize the value of the 'whole' person and not just what the culture dictates makes us valuable; we are more than our bodies and achievements. She believes in the integration of the whole person.

Her dream is that these schools not only empower men and women but that they also equip them with practical tools to live a fulfilling life, a life fully alive.

She teaches that we have a universal call to inspire people, so we can create a ripple impact in our homes, our communities, our relationships, and our careers. We change the world by changing our interior world first.

As a wife and mother of eight children, January is fierce about integrating business and motherhood. She reminds her students that our professional dreams ought to be integrated with our personal dreams; we just need to *train-up* for them.

January believes that success cannot be void of fulfillment, because our hearts are made for it.

DEDICATION

I would like to dedicate this book to the people who have accompanied me on my own fulfillment journey.

My Husband, Ryan
You are my everything. You make all my dreams possible. Life with you is beautiful and it just keeps getting better. Thank you for the many ways you make me feel valued. I am who I am because of the way you love me. You've set my heart free. I love you forever and always. You are home to me.

My Children
You make motherhood so sweet. You teach me so much about life. Thank you for the deep joy you've brought to my heart. It is an honor to watch you grow. I am forever grateful for the life you give me. I cherish each one of you...thank you for helping me become the woman I want to be.

My Family
Mom, thank you for your courage and sacrifice.
Brother, thank you for making me laugh and for carrying me through my struggles.
Sister, thank you for always listening and for loving me as I am.
Dad, thank you for believing in me when I didn't believe in myself. You are my first love.

The Woman School Community
Thank you for joining this Call. Your witness humbles and inspires me. I am honored to be fighting alongside you. It is a privilege to serve you.

My Mentors

Elena, without you, The Woman School would not exist. Thank you for awakening the call that was ordained for me. To all my mentors, thank you for helping me achieve my impossible dreams and helping me develop a life of discipline.

Our Lord

Thank You for Your mercy. All that I am I owe to You. All that I am is for You. May I never separate from Your Love.

FULFILLMENT FORMULA
Formula to Becoming Fully Alive

- Discover the dream of the season.
- Design every part of your life in the context of the Dream.
- Decide who you need to become to achieve the Dream and Design.

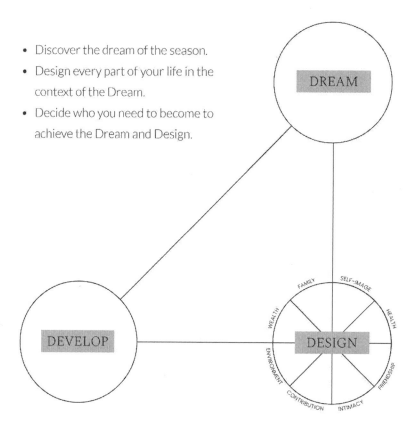

CONTENTS

PROLOGUE xv
Introduction xxi

Chapter 1: Am I Successful? 1
   1. An Honest Assessment of Your Life 1
   2. You Are Not Alone 4
   3. "The Poisonous P's" – the Metric For Success 8
   4. What Does Success Mean For Me Right Now? 17
   5. Asking Hard Questions 19
   6. Redefining Success: Moving From Achievement to Fulfillment 23
   7. This Book is for You if... 23
   8. This Book is Your Blueprint to Redefining Your Success as a Woman 26

Chapter 2: Success Begins With Knowing What You Want 28
   1. Success Cannot Be Apart From What You Want 28
   2. What Do You Not Want to Put Up With Anymore? ... 32
   3. The Wholeness Arena 35
   4. Roadblocks to Getting What You Want 49
   5. Consequences of Ignoring or Indulging in What you Want 58
   6. The 10 Universal Desires that Unite Women 61
   7. The Purpose of Focusing on What You Want 69

Chapter 3: Success Must Be Rooted In Fulfillment 73
   1. The Old Model of Success Does Not Work 73
   2. Why Do We Need to Redefine Success for Women? ... 75
   3. The Purpose of a Successful Life 79
   4. Guideposts to Redefining Success 82
   5. The Fulfillment Formula 101
   6. The New Model of Success is Rooted in Fulfillment ... 105
   7. Unfulfilled People Become Toxic to Our Community ... 107
   8. How to Begin to Design a Fulfilling Life 108

Chapter 4: Success Requires a Dream **111**
  1. Dreams vs. Goals 114
  2. Why is it Important to Fulfill Your Dream? 127
  3. What is the Dream of the Season? 129
  4. Three Reasons Why Women Are Not Dreaming 130
  5. What if I Have Never Had a Dream? 132
  6. How to Discover Your Dream Now 132

Chapter 5: SUCCESS REQUIRES A LIFE BY DESIGN **141**
  1. Old Belief = "You Can't Have What You Want" 142
  2. Why Skill is the Bridge to Having It All 146
  3. What Does "Having It All" Mean To You? 155
  4. Ground Rules For Designing a Life of Wholeness 159
  5. Designing a Life that is Whole 164
  6. Fulfillment is Your Choice 221

Chapter 6: SUCCESS REQUIRES YOU TO DESIGN YOU ... **224**
  1. Information is Not Formation 225
  2. Success Requires You to Design a Whole New
     Version of You 228
  3. Your Fulfillment is Your Responsibility, and
     Discipline is the Secret Sauce 234
  4. Train-Up For the Life You Want 242
  5. The Cost of an Underdeveloped Self 244
  6. Rules and Freedom 245
  7. 21 Rules For Women 251

Chapter 7: Success is Your Choice **284**
  1. Nothing Changes Your Value 284
  2. Our Differences Should Not Divide Us 295
  3. Where Do You Go From Here? 297
  4. Redefine Success For You 303
  5. My Hope For You 307

EPILOGUE: A Call to Rise Together **313**

PROLOGUE

I decided to go for the "unsuccessful" life.

My mom was ambitious and fierce.
She fought her way to success.

When she was seven years old, her mother left her and her seven siblings to be with another man.

So my mom started helping her father by selling peanuts in the slums of the Philippines. She was a fighter, she had no choice.

Her mother abandoned her. Her family was broken. She didn't have a place to call home, and life around her was complete chaos. She lived only to survive.

She endured so much pain as a little girl. But, her suffering became the fuel that made her a successful woman.Success was her escape. She fought her way through a very hard life to have a shot at success. She was determined to be successful at all costs.

For her, success meant escaping not only poverty but also the pain of a broken family and a broken heart. She suffered through it all. But, she made it.

She built a lucrative company and became the successful woman she had always wanted to be.

She was a classic story of rags to riches.
She escaped.

But.

She was miserable.
Everyone around her felt miserable.

Her marriage was unbearable to watch as a child.
She was lonely.
She felt guilt, and shame, and blamed herself.

She felt the constant need to prove her worth. It was exhausting to watch her climb the ladder of 'never enough.'

She hated herself.
She hated her life.
She numbed herself.

But in the eyes of the world, she was a success story.

There were a lot of tears for me growing up.
I barely knew her. I barely saw her.
I don't know what it is like to have a mom tuck you into bed.
I don't know what it is like to have a mom who aches to be with her daughter.

I cried for her, I cried for me, and I cried for us.
I cried as a little girl because the successful life she wanted was void of me.

I was not part of her success.

She achieved the success she wanted, but she lost herself in the process. And she lost me.

Her ambition to do "the next big thing" blinded her to the present moment, when I needed her most. I needed my mommy to not be successful so she could be with me.

But she desperately wanted to prove to everyone that she was no longer a little girl from the slums. She was now a successful woman.

But.

The price of success was high.
I was the price.
Her marriage was the price.
Her peace of mind was the price.
Her life was the price for success.

But.

It was not her fault.
She needed success to survive.
No one showed her any other way.
She did the best that she could with what she knew then.
Despite the odds, she found the courage to protect us from her past.

In her eyes, her success was her gift to us.

The truth is, my mother has a heart of gold. She desperately wanted to feel valued, and success made her feel valuable.

To her, this quest for success and tremendous achievement meant that she was finally worthy of being seen and heard.

Success was her way to prove to the world that her life mattered. Deep inside, all she wanted was to love and be loved.

She wanted a beautiful marriage and a beautiful family because she was robbed of this as a child.

She wanted to have a loving home because she never knew what home was like.

She wanted wealth because she didn't know where her next meal would come from.

She chose success because she believed that success would fill the void of her unfulfilled heart. But it didn't.

She hated her successful life.

But I am grateful for what she endured. I've learned so much. She showed me how to fight for what I wanted.

I am who I am because of the woman she CHOSE to become.

Her wounds became the compass for my contribution to this world. Without her pain, I would not have endured the pain I needed to, in order to fuel my unique call.

Her life became the foundation on which I would make choices for my life.

I wanted nothing to do with success.
I gave up success—it was not an option I gave myself.

I decided to go for the "unsuccessful life" because I didn't want her life to be my life.

I wanted nothing to do with success. I wanted a loving family, a beautiful marriage, quality friendships, and a place I could call home.

I wanted a simple life that was meaningful, and full of joy and peace. I wanted to be fully alive.

In my own limited mind, I wanted what she didn't have. But in doing so, I ignored the deepest desires of my heart.

I declined success for a shot at fulfillment.

The irony of this is that my mother chose success so she, too, could have a shot at a fulfilling life.

We chose two different paths to search for the same destination... fulfillment.

Sadly, most women today are unfulfilled.

Over the past twenty years, I've been on a quest to discover what makes women feel successful.

The book you hold in your hands is the result of decades of research, study, teaching, coaching, tears, prayer, failure, and determination, to find out how to overcome our limiting beliefs of what a successful woman is and to begin the journey of redefining success that is rooted in what we all want...fulfillment.

Regardless of what you choose to do with your life, we all share a universal desire written in the deepest part of our hearts to achieve a fulfilling life. It is about living a life that is whole, where every part of our life feels abundant.

Success, therefore, cannot be void of fulfillment.

This book will give you practical tools to redefine success for you, both personally and professionally.

It is about you taking responsibility for your own fulfillment.
This book is about getting what you really really want while also tasting the joy that comes from getting what you want without sacrificing parts of yourself.

This book will give you a blueprint that integrates both success and fulfillment.

It is not either or, it is a both/and.

I will show you how.

INTRODUCTION

I vowed to myself that I never wanted a "successful" life.

I didn't want money.
I didn't want fame.
I didn't want to be a bad mom.
I didn't want a hard marriage.
I didn't want to lose my faith.
I didn't want to be part of the Who's Who Club.
I didn't want to become my mother.

The pain I endured as a child influenced my perception of the price women pay to pursue a successful life. It was impressed upon me that success *and* happiness were not possible. Therefore, I had to choose one or the other.

- I would rather be happy than be successful.
- I would rather have a happy family than be successful.
- I would rather have a happy marriage than be successful.
- I would rather be peaceful than be successful.
- I would rather be a nobody if it meant I could be happy.
- I would rather stay small than be unfulfilled.
- I would rather be happy than have money.

So, I chose an unsuccessful life in exchange for a happier life.

I had subconsciously defined success as the extreme opposite of a beautiful and meaningful life. Success, to me, meant chaos and hardship, and I wanted nothing to do with it.

But I was wrong.
This book is about making things right.

Right for you, right for me, and right for all women.
This is about fighting for true freedom and taking off the shackles that have kept us small and insignificant.

It is about breaking the false narrative of conflicting views that no longer serve us.

This is about a generational fight for the hearts of women now and for generations to come.
This is about creating your legacy.
This is about ownership of who you were created to be.

We no longer have to spend years of our life having to prove that we are worthy of what is good.

Enough is enough.
It is time to rise up.
We can no longer afford to sit back.

We must reclaim our worth and take back what was stolen from us.

This book is about fighting the real war against women; the war that has been waged against us and within us.

Make no mistake, there is a battle against our worth.

You are fighting it every day whether you realize it or not.

Chances are, you are feeling the mental exhaustion from being devalued by a culture that has created a false metric of what deems a woman valuable.

You have to make it stop—for yourself.
We have to join hearts and minds and put a stop to this madness.

We have to start fighting for each other.
We have to acknowledge our pain and weep for wounds that have made our hearts heavy. And then, we dry our tears and allow our pain to be the armor for the battle ahead.

In this battle you fight for your worth, because you are the first woman you fight for.

There is a new freedom that is worthy of the fight, the freedom to believe that we are worthy of what is good, true, and beautiful.

Your time is now.
Because now could be your only time.

Ask yourself:

- *Have I chosen a successful or unsuccessful life?*
- *Am I fulfilled as a woman?*
- *Do I believe that fulfillment and success ought to be integrated? Or, is it one or the other? Why?*
- *Do I believe in both/and—both a successful and fulfilling life?*
- *How do I define success right now?*
- *Have I made up my mind that success is not possible for me?*

You don't have to answer right now.

I want to take you on a journey of redefining what success means for you.

You get to decide.

I will clarify the distinction between a *successful* and a *fulfilling* life.

This book is about *your* personal and professional fulfillment, this is about creating a life of wholeness. Wholeness means that *every part of your life is fulfilled* and not just parts of you.

This is not just about balance, but rather, the integration of all your desires.

This book is about abundance.
Abundance, as we define it, is being in a perpetual state of gratitude and generosity.

This book is about getting what you want and no longer putting up with what you don't want. It is about discovering the deepest most sacred desires of your heart.

This book is about believing in your irreplaceable purpose.

My goal is for you to redefine what success looks like for you, and more importantly, what it feels like. Achieving success that is void of fulfillment cannot be a sustainable metric for success.

Success, therefore, needs to be redefined in order to create a sustainable metric that brings more life to women, not robs them of it.

As you cruise through this book, journal your way through the insights and questions. See yourself and own your success story.

This is about you redefining yourself and your future.
What I am going to reveal to you could flip your world upside down, or maybe, just maybe, the right side up.

This book is about fighting for women's true fulfillment, giving all women a shot at a successful and fulfilling life.

My personal goal is for you to design your success story and begin the work necessary to achieve it.

In the first part, I bring awareness to what makes a woman fulfilled and unfulfilled by giving you language for what you want and don't want.

Chances are, you are feeling the angst of restlessness, resentment, and anxiety that come from unfulfillment, but you can't put your finger on why parts of you feel empty.

Language is the battlefield.

I want to give you language for the wounds you have incurred from having to constantly prove your worth to the people who disapprove of you.

When you give language to both your struggle and your deepest desires, then half the battle has been won.

We will finally learn to be free from the prison of comparison that has pinned us against each other. We will identify the real enemy.

The second part of the book is about designing your life based on a new definition of success that integrates your fulfillment and your unique purpose in the world. I will give you specific exercises to walk through deeper layers of awareness and understanding. You will get to make your own rules for your success.

The ball of success is in your court.

I want to convince you that your worth is unconditional; you are not for sale.

You can't squander your value.

I want to convince you that your value does not change.

Regardless of...
...anyone else's opinion of you.
...your success or lack thereof.
...your fame or fortune, or lack thereof.
...the extra PhD in your name or lack thereof.
...how many people follow you or unfollow you.
...how many people like you or hate you.
...your performance or what you can produce.

Not even your opinion of yourself changes your value.
Your value is irrevocable.

Nothing changes your value, nothing.

You are valuable simply because you exist.
You are unrepeatable, therefore, what you offer this world is irreplaceable.

No one can be you.

Your life begins to unleash when you understand, from a very deep level, that your value is unchanging.

I want to show you that your purpose has everything to do with knowing your worth.

Some of the concepts I will be teaching can be hard and could possibly break your heart—they broke mine. But if you give them a chance to penetrate your heart, they will heal you, and eventually, give you wings to fly.

This book will make you reflect on how you've lived every part of your life so far.

It will give you permission to restore parts of you that you might have ignored.

It might sting a little—or a lot—but it will give you hope that in the remaining days of your life, you can achieve the fulfilling life you've always wanted...as long as you are willing to *Train-Up* for it.
You can have it all (wholeness) and actually enjoy it all.

This book is a journey to discovering a whole new version of you.

My goal is to shatter the old narrative that success is only available for the exclusive .000001% of women.

No one should go through life doubting their own success.
By redefining success for women, we give all women a shot at success.

We are all different and uniquely created, therefore our success cannot be the same. But it should feel the same...fulfilling.

No one else can define success for you.
You have to redefine it for yourself.
This book is your blueprint for redefining success.

You get to write and rewrite your story now.

This is about your life, your story, and how you choose to live it.
You are responsible for yourself.

When you make the decision to take responsibility for your fulfillment, the sky's the limit.

You can have it all while enjoying it all.

You can be a whole version of yourself.

Let's begin.

IMPORTANT NOTES BEFORE YOU BEGIN

- *Throughout this book, you will see "PPA" reminders (like the graphic below). These are reminders to "PAUSE, PONDER, AND ACT" on the information and actions steps provided.*

- *Whenever you see this symbol let it serve as a reminder to take action on what you are learning.*

- *Taking action is an absolute must for your transformation. I am making this crystal clear for you because there is no transformation without application. You must PAUSE, PONDER, AND ACT on what you learn in order to experience the transformation that awaits you.*

- *Be sure to take full advantage of the tremendous free resources provided for you throughout this book.*

- *Visit redefinesuccessforwomen.com for more information and to access the free resources.*

- *Be a woman of massive action!*

CHAPTER 1

AM I SUCCESSFUL?

1. An Honest Assessment
2. You Are Not Alone
3. "The Poisonous P's" – the Metric For Success
4. What Does Success Mean For Me Right Now?
5. Asking Hard Questions
6. Redefining Success: Moving From Achievement to Fulfillment
7. This Book is for You if...
8. This Book is Your Blueprint to Redefining Your Success as a Woman

An Honest Assessment of Your Life

It is not always easy to have an honest, heart-to-heart conversation with yourself. It requires so much courage to ask hard questions about where you currently are in your life.

Asking these questions means you might need to cry, scream, and feel the angst of realizing you are not living the life you actually want.

Ask yourself, "Do I feel successful?"

Having worked with thousands of women, I know that there is a good chance your answer would be *no*.

Most of the time, life is so busy that there is simply no time to pause and ponder some of the most important questions: questions about who you are, about what you're doing, about your purpose in life.

"Busyness" becomes an excuse to avoid sitting with painful questions that could unearth old wounds of resentment. It hurts to look at yourself in the mirror and not like the woman staring back.

For some of us, we look in the mirror and under our breath, we say, "I hate myself." Then we go about our day, serving everyone else from a cup that is empty.

Frankly, it is easier to numb ourselves rather than to face hard questions about a job we hate, constant stress, our exhausted bodies, the emotional roller coaster, the chaos in our home, the marriage that is falling apart, and children who may not be growing up to be wholesome individuals. It is easier to not deal with the fact that parts of our life feel so broken. It hurts too much.

When we don't face hard questions, we numb ourselves to the compounding pain that could eventually make us feel overwhelmed, burnt out, anxious, restless, angry, resentful, and full of self-doubt. This is why we scroll through other people's online posts, comparing a life we hate to the glorious filtered life of social media. No wonder so many women feel trapped in the prison of comparison—it is pure self-imposed torture.

But just because we don't deal with the pain, doesn't mean we are not burdened by it. The truth is, we feel the ache, regardless of whether or not we have language for it.

It is like a tumor growing in the body—we can only ignore it for so long until it spreads. Eventually, we have to deal with it.

For example, a bad marriage impacts our career, our children, our self-image, and our mental, emotional, physical, and spiritual health. When parts of our life are toxic, it is only a matter of time before everything else becomes toxic.

But there is good news! Unlike cancer, where it can feel too late, it is not too late for you. You can heal, and rewrite your story.

> "The quality of our questions determines the quality of our lives." -Tony Robbins

It begins with asking yourself hard questions that punch you in the gut. They will bring clarity to the source of your pain so that you can heal from within and not just treat symptoms that eventually won't be contained.

By answering hard questions, you have a chance to come face to face with parts of yourself that have hardened from years of compounding heartaches and disappointments.

It may not be your fault that parts of your life feel broken, but it is your responsibility to fix them moving forward. If you want a shot at happiness, you have to take responsibility for your life.

There are many external circumstances that you just can't control, but you don't have to be a victim of them.

You can defy them, or rather, redefine them, by harvesting what is good.

No matter your brokenness, there is always hope until your last breath. This is the only life you have, and it is worth the fight.

You are here in this moment of history with all the unique circumstances that come with being alive at this moment. Not only are you living in a unique combination of time and circumstance, but you are an unrepeatable woman who has an irreplaceable contribution to offer to this world, in this moment of history. This combination is powerful evidence that what you offer the world, no one else can.

No one can be you and no one can do it as you do it.

When you take responsibility for your life, you will begin the journey of discovering your unique call; the very purpose for why you are here on earth.

You Are Not Alone

After working with thousands of women across forty countries over the past two decades, I want to tell you that *you are not alone in your pain.*

Women today are aching from unfulfillment but we don't talk about it, partly because we don't know how to talk about it.

Unfulfillment means that parts of your life are not how you want them to be, and they are depleting you.

Maybe you are in a marriage where you have to prove your value and you have accepted that as your norm, even though it hurts you every day.

Maybe you are in a toxic work environment where you feel belittled and degraded, but you don't think there is anything you can do about it. So you put up with it and feel worthless every day. And your children can feel it, too.

Maybe you hate your body and you tell yourself that every day. You avoid the camera, the mirror, and the scale because they are constant reminders of how much you can't stand yourself.

Maybe your friendships are shallow and you can't trust that your current friends won't gossip about you. But you put up with it because you are lonely and you've convinced yourself that it is better to have toxic friendships than ache for loneliness. But somehow, you still feel lonely.

You feel like you are a broken mess, even though you've fought so hard, day in and day out. You are tired, depleted, and barely surviving throughout the day.

A big problem is that we don't clarify how a toxic career impacts your home life. Or how your home life impacts your self-image. And how self-image impacts your friendships.

Every part of you is impacted.

The unfulfillment that you are feeling in certain areas of your life bleeds into every part of you. You are not a compartmentalized human being, you are integrated.

Whatever pain you are feeling in parts of you will eventually be felt by every part of you.

This is a big culprit in our burnout culture.

We have to identify the real enemy that is costing us the life we want, otherwise, we will continue to hand over the same mental overwhelm to the next generation.

The cycle continues to repeat itself. And unfulfilled women can become toxic to their community.

Why? *Because hurt people hurt other people.*

Unfulfilled women cannot fill other people's cups; that is an illusion. You can't give what you don't have.

You can't fight for peace unless you are peaceful.
You can't bring positivity from a negative mindset.
You can't bring good to the world when you don't see what good is within you.

Frankly, it is easier to solve the world's problems rather than our own interior problems.

It doesn't matter what we accomplish externally if we are broken interiorly.
We can't enjoy what we achieve.
It won't even matter if we "have it all," if we can't enjoy any of it at all.

It is unsustainable.

There is no joy in our great achievements when we have no one to celebrate them with.
Success can be a very lonely road of achievement when it is void of fulfillment.
This is why we need to dig deep into what makes a woman fulfilled or unfulfilled.

Our achievements ought to bring us joy.
But, we can't share the joy that we don't have. Even when we want to.

We can't fake joy.
We can't fake peace.

We can't fake fulfillment.

Even if you can fool everyone else, you can't fool yourself.

Your light will grow dim.
Your heart will grow cold.
Your life will be void of life.

Today, women are living their life with no life.

Alive with no life inside.

But, you are not alone in your battle.
Most of us are suffering in the quiet of our thoughts.
After over twenty years of having a front-row seat to women's tears, I cannot help but see the collective ache that is causing so much depletion and depression.

As Henry David Thoreau says, "The mass of men lead lives of quiet desperation."

Women are desperate for more life.

There is a war against us, but it is a cunning war because it is a silent war. It is a war waged against our interior freedom, attacking us from within, that is contributing to the rage within us. However you slice it, we are not free, free to be fully alive.

We are not free to live in joy and peace.
We are not free when we are in a state of having to constantly prove our value. And the reality is that many of us are being devalued in our homes, at work, and pretty much everywhere else.

There is no true freedom when our worth is conditional.

This is a war against our worth.

"The Poisonous P's" – the Metric For Success

There is a false metric of success—based solely on achievement—that is costing us dearly. The western world is plagued by high statistics of burnout, stress, anxiety, and depression. Burnout affects over 70% of employees. Over forty million adults in the US have an anxiety disorder, and over 10.5% of women suffer from depression.

This is unjust.

What good is achieving the world if we lose parts of who we are?

What is the root cause of so many women suffering today?

Is it possible that the root cause of our pain stems from a culture in which women are conditioned to prove that they are worthy of acceptance and belonging?

We have a primary and universal need for belonging. It is written in our hearts. So we do everything we can for a chance to belong, even if it costs us our peace. We have acquired the need to prove ourselves because of our human ache to survive.

We crave belonging because we are made for it.

Women are lured into pursuing a successful life so they can prove that they are worthy of belonging.

But we end up proving this based only on our achievements, which devalues the woman.

Yet, because women have an innate need to belong, we hustle to prove ourselves. The current metric of success exacerbates the need for women to prove themselves.

We call this metric of success, **"The Poisonous P's."**

It is a metric of success that poisons our fulfillment. These five Poisonous P's have become the universal metric for a successful woman. We don't question them, we just believe them.

Figure 1.1

POISONOUS P'S

"POISONOUS P" IS POISON TO OUR FULFILLMENT

P1 : POWER

P2 : PRESTIGE

P3 : POSSESSION   POISONOUS METRIC FOR SUCCESS

P4 : POPULARITY

P5 : PERFECTION

Go to redefinesuccessforwomen.com for a free printable download.

P1: POWER—Success means, "I am in a powerful position, I am important."

P2: PRESTIGE—Success means, "I have achieved prestige, therefore, I am more significant."

P3: POSSESSION—Success means, "I have possessions that make me better than everyone else."

P4: POPULARITY—Success means, "I am famous, I am now worthy of appreciation."

P5: PERFECTION—Success means, "My life is perfect, so I am worthy of admiration."

This false metric of success is really a cry for significance.

We feel valued when we feel significant, therefore we have created a lifestyle of proving our significance.

We have created an external metric for success that has led to women proving their value. Achievement has become their god.

This is poisonous.

According to dictionary.com, the definition of success is, "The accomplishment of one's goals. The attainment of wealth, position, and honors."

But this definition does not consider how a woman feels as a result of accomplishing her goals.

When we define success as exclusive to achievement alone and void of the fulfillment that we desire, then it feels like we have forgotten our basic need to feel valued.

When we force a metric of success that is solely based on what a woman can produce, we promote a culture that devalues the woman.

This current metric of success leads us to conclude that: A woman is only worthy if and when she can prove to the world that she has the power, prestige, possession, popularity, and perfection that we have come to revere.

This metric of success is poisoning everyone's ability to see *her* and her unchangeable value.

Not even she knows her value, apart from this metric.

It's toxic!

We are more than our bodies and our achievements.

We are women with hearts that bleed, hurt, and are wounded by having to constantly prove ourselves.

We are not the sum of our money or our possessions. We are far more valuable than any jewel and yet, we hope to wear the biggest diamond so we can feel important in the room.

No wonder so many of us feel unfulfilled! We are constantly in the rat race of proving ourselves.

Why can't we just acknowledge that every woman is valuable and significant regardless of what she achieves?

Is being alive not enough to prove that we matter?

Is the fact that we are irreplaceable and unrepeatable human beings enough proof of our value?

Clearly not.

Whether you realize it or not, most likely this false metric of success has convinced you to choose a successful or an unsuccessful life.

This poisonous metric has pushed you to exhaustion.

Or, it has made you feel unworthy of being a part of an exclusive club that seems to be only available for .000001% of women.

It is poisoning us because an achievement void of meaning does not fulfill you.

It is poisonous because it is leading us to division, fueling unhealthy comparison and competition that hinder our need for collaboration and unity.

It is poison because it bleeds into all the different arenas of our life until eventually, we feel like we can't keep going anymore. We are too burnt out.

What looks successful, doesn't always feel successful.

Women are tired of having to constantly prove their value. Every day we fight the same battles, trying to demonstrate that we are good enough for someone—for anyone—and this causes mental and emotional exhaustion.

Imagine a soldier who cannot get up to wield her sword.
A woman who feels defeated in battle time and time again eventually loses her will to fight. She can only get pummeled for so long until her heart grows weary.

What does this battle look like today?

An unhappy woman, endlessly scrolling through social media, comparing her life to everyone else's.

It looks like waiting for Friday to live and dreading Monday morning.

It looks like holding your breath for retirement because you've spent most of your life unfulfilled and you can't wait to free yourself from this cage of unfulfillment.

This looks like a woman giving up on her physical and mental health; overdrinking, overshopping, overeating, or using other addictions to numb her pain.

It looks like a mother who is angry and easily frustrated with her children because she is actually frustrated with herself.

It looks like a woman who is angry at everyone else's success because deep inside, she wants to be successful, but doesn't know how.

It looks like a mid-life crisis; a woman trying to use external goods to fulfill her internal needs. But it does not work. The temporary satisfaction she experiences does not last, because deep inside there is a woman who is aching to be valued just as she is.

It feels like regret, guilt, shame, and anger.

It feels painful.

Maybe this battle-weary soldier is your friend, your co-worker, your daughter, your sister, your cousin, your mother, and maybe even your grandmother.

Perhaps, this woman is you.

Is it your fault that you could be trapped in a life of proving and pleasing?

I say No. I say that we have been poisoned.

We have been conditioned to believe that "success" is determined solely by achieving the things that our society deems to be important.

This means that unless we achieve these five Ps, we do not qualify as "successful." This metric, then, disqualifies teachers, mothers, empty nesters, policewomen, and hard-working women who earn below minimum wage. It disqualifies most of us.

Our current metric of success is defined by how well we can prove our value based on our possessions, power, prestige, popularity, and perfection. This is an unsustainable model for success.

This is why we need a new metric for success.
If we are to empower women, then we first need to help them understand that their worth is unconditional.

It all begins with seeing that nothing changes our value.

You are not for sale.
You are priceless.

Ask yourself:

- *Am I impressed with women who have fancy cars, clothes, and fancy homes? Why?*
- *Do I revere women who have large social media followings? Do I feel less important than them?*
- *Do I feel insecure around women who have PhDs or high-paying jobs? Do I exclude myself from work events or parties that make me feel insecure?*
- *Am I repelled by women who look like they have a "perfect" life? Does it make me jealous deep inside?*

Whatever your feelings are, they are valid.

Hang in there...we are going to work on this.

If we tell women that success is simply rooted in achievement, what we are promoting is for women to numb their deepest desires to live a fulfilling life; a life that gives them more life.

Success that is defined by mere achievement alone is void of what women truly want—a life full of life—to be fully alive.

I am not suggesting that we stop our ability to accomplish great things in life, but what I am suggesting is to shift our focus to *achieving fulfillment while in pursuit of what we want to achieve,* and not just blindly follow what our culture has pressured us to achieve.

We can't continue to empower women to become successful by giving up fulfillment. What I am proposing is that we redefine success to integrate both achievement and fulfillment.

In addition, we cannot disregard the journey.

What I am boldly claiming here is that we can have both/and, not one or the other. We can achieve great things while also being fulfilled. We can achieve not only great accomplishments, but we can also enjoy the journey. That would be amazing.

For us to be fulfilled, we have to achieve the things that we feel called to achieve, while prioritizing our need for fulfillment. Achieving fulfillment is the primary goal.

True success, then, has to be rooted in pursuing fulfillment first. The path to achieving our goals should be equally as rewarding as the journey of getting there. The means have to justify the ends.

Why? Because...
Money without peace might look grand, but it won't make you happy.

The **fame** that leads to constant self-doubt might look glamorous, but it will feel like a mental roller coaster.

Popularity void of quality friendships might look impressive, but it will breed loneliness.

A **prestigious** title that causes you to feel burnt out, guilty as a mom, or puts a strain on your marriage, might look great on the outside, but you will feel like an imposter inside.

Possession, power, prestige, popularity, and perfection are plaguing women, driving them toward a life of unfulfillment.

These "markers of success" are poisonous because this metric has pushed us to a point of exhaustion, all for the sake of a shot at a "successful" life.

We are chasing success for all the wrong reasons.

> If your current definition of success looks like the script below, then perhaps you have to wrestle with understanding your unconditional worth. Work through the scripts below. Ask yourself why you answered in this way.
>
> P1: POWER. "I am successful if and when I achieve _____."
> P2: PRESTIGE. "I am successful if and when I achieve _____."
> P3: POSSESSION. "I am successful if and when I achieve _____."
> P4: POPULARITY. "I am successful if and when I achieve _____."
> P5: PERFECTION. "I am successful if and when I achieve _____."

In the next few chapters, we are going to replace this false metric of success, so hang tight.

There is hope.

I believe it is time for us to start a national conversation about this war against women's worth. We must replace the poisonous metric of success that is causing us to doubt our value.

No more proving, no more pleasing, and no more accepting lies.
It is time we fight for each other.

This is about a generational movement to heal from the past, rewrite the present, and embolden the future of all women. We have the opportunity, and a duty, to change the trajectory for women in the future.

What Does Success Mean For Me Right Now?

To begin the journey of redefining success for you, you first need to understand how you are currently defining success.

Answer the following questions:

- Describe a successful woman. Who comes to mind? Does she have a nice house, a million dollars, a perfect body, perfect children, and a spotless home? Is she a doctor or a teacher? Who is she to you? Name her. Describe her.
- Is someone with one million followers more important than someone who has 100 followers on social media?

Who came to mind?
Was it you?

- What does an unsuccessful woman look like? What does her presence feel like? Describe her. What does she like or not like about herself?

Who came to mind?
Is she you?

There are no right or wrong answers, they just reveal how you have been conditioned to believe what a successful woman should look like.

Now, to a deeper question.

- How does a successful woman feel? Imagine how she feels, then describe it. Is she peaceful? Is she full of joy? Is she humble? Confident, resilient, kind, disciplined, sincere, strong? Or, is she a bully? Rude, reckless, frivolous, materialistic, entitled, prideful, and thinks only of herself, aka, selfish? Is she overwhelmed, frustrated, bitter, or a ball of stress?

The point of this exercise is that we have all made judgments on what success ought to look like, but maybe we have not considered what it is supposed to feel like.

The point of this imagination exercise is to uncover your perception of a successful woman. Your definition will tell you so much about your own pursuit of success.

- Do you want to see yourself as a successful woman?
- Are you currently pursuing success at all costs because you believe that success will fulfill you? Or, are you avoiding success out of a fear of being unfulfilled?

Do you desire a life that has so much life that you feel alive every day?
Have you ever acknowledged your desire to be fully alive?
This is what it feels like to be fulfilled.

It doesn't mean you won't have struggles. But it does mean that even in your struggle, your cup remains full. You carry a deep peace within you and your cup overflows.

We want peace. We want joy. We want more in our life.

Redefining success that is rooted in fulfillment gives every woman a shot at success.

As we now know, the current "poisonous" metric for a successful woman, based solely on achievement, is unsustainable. If we want to create a world where women are full of life, then we need to replace the old metric of success—shifting from achievement to fulfillment. In doing so, we can create a national conversation of redefining success with this new metric—fulfillment—rather than achievement.

If we don't, we will continue to have a sad, cruel world full of unfulfilled women.

We are experiencing a generational crisis of unfulfilled women who doubt their value, and we need a new movement to fight against it.

It is time for you to fight against it. And we begin the fight by asking some hard questions.

Asking Hard Questions

You can't free yourself from a prison unless you know you are in one.

My mentor's words always ring true, "Let it hurt January, don't numb yourself from the pain. Feel it, because that is how you heal from it."

If you dare to feel the ache of answering hard questions, then you have a shot at fulfillment. You won't have to risk waking up one day with knots in your stomach because you feel trapped in a life you hate. But if you don't face these questions, you risk regret.

When we do not change, we remain the same woman week after week and year after year. We start to feel anxious and wonder if we are wasting our life. We feel unsuccessful, unaccomplished, and unfulfilled.

Now, you may not be using exactly those words to define how you feel, but chances are, you are feeling the anxiety that comes with it, regardless if you have words to describe it.

The fact that we feel a level of restlessness about our life is a signal that we should dig a little deeper, find its source and address it before we erupt like a pent-up volcano causing turmoil and devastation to everything it touches. Let's face these things before we face a crisis that impacts every part of our life.

We want to avoid finding ourselves asking, "How did this happen?"

> "The quality of your life is a direct reflection of the quality of the questions you are asking yourself." –Tony Robbins

So…are you ready?

Let's take an honest inventory of your life right now.

Caution: these questions could hurt. But it is better to ask them now before it's too late.

If this process doesn't feel good, that's okay—it usually feels worse before it feels better. That is how we heal from the inside out.

You can journal or process these questions with a trusted guide, but make sure you can trust them with vulnerable information. Your heart is sacred, so do not squander it with people who have not earned the right to be in your sacred space.

Questions:

1. Do I like who I am right now? Why or why not?
2. Do I feel fulfilled and inspired every day, regardless of my current circumstances? Why or why not?
3. Am I intentionally designing every part of my life based on what I want and don't want (not based on what everyone else thinks I should want)?
4. Do I have a clear dream that I am pursuing that scares me and excites me at the same time?
5. Am I intentionally designing and developing myself to become the woman I want to be six months from now?

These answers should be a window to your own fulfillment. If your answer is a resounding "Yes!" to these questions, consider yourself lucky. Most women can't say yes to these questions because they have not been taught to ask them at all.

Let's continue with a quick assessment, rating your success journey. Rate yourself 0 - 10; 10 being a resounding "Yes," 0 being a brutal "No."

RATE YOUR SUCCESS JOURNEY: 0-10

1. I feel successful as a woman right now.
2. I wholeheartedly believe that my value as a woman is not determined by my accomplishments. I have nothing to prove and no one to please.
3. I believe success requires me to value and integrate every part of my life and not just parts of me. I am more than my body or achievements.
4. I believe in my unique and irreplaceable contribution to this world. I have no need to compare myself to other women.
5. I am intentionally designing every part of my life, and working toward fulfilling the deepest desires of my heart.
6. I love the woman I am becoming, with all my imperfections and failures, because I am intentionally growing in harmony with who I was created to be.

Whatever your answers, honor your journey! The first step toward healing is recognizing what parts of you are hurting. In this situation, pain is actually a gift, because it brings awareness to what we need healing from.

Over the next few chapters, I will walk you through a discovery process that will build off of these questions. We will ponder and reveal the deepest desires of your heart, which might have been silenced by those around you. We are going to break down how you got here, and uncover what it is that you really want. So hang tight, as these chapters are carefully crafted for you to journey through your own story.

My goal for you is to take a full inventory of every part of your life so you can redefine success based on what fulfills you. This will require you to dig deeper, and determine what YOU want and don't want in every part of your life (not what everyone else thinks you should want).

You cannot taste the sweet joy of fulfillment by subscribing to everyone else's opinion, or the culture's current metric.
Your journey to fulfillment is unique to you.
No one can design it for you, you have to own it.

I will show you how.

Every woman should have an equal shot at becoming a successful woman. Everyone. Whatever profession you are in, you deserve to feel successful. By redefining what success means for you, you will no longer feel insecure. You can have a seat at the table.

Each woman has the equal opportunity to become the artist of her own life. Your life is your art. No one else should paint it for you, and nor can they, because what is inside of you can only be fully understood by you. You get to paint for yourself.

And once you find that fulfillment—that success—this art in which you live your life can become the inspiration that inspires other women to become the artist of their own life.

It is up to you to create this masterpiece, this art, the art of being a successful woman.

Redefining Success: Moving From Achievement to Fulfillment

We owe it to ourselves to redefine success based on our own terms.

Redefining success requires us to integrate achievement with fulfillment. Because, what good is achieving the world if we are losing parts of ourselves?

To feel fulfilled, you must achieve the things you have sought out to achieve AND pursue what you want in your life—not what everyone else thinks you should want. At the same time, you can't simply focus on achievement alone, void of what fulfills you.

Redefining success is about the integration of achieving your dreams and your deepest desires while intentionally designing a life that fulfills you in the process. It is a both/and situation.

Based on the Merriam Dictionary definition, being fulfilled means, "Feeling happiness and satisfaction. Feeling that one's abilities and talents are being fully used."

Furthermore, being fulfilled means that we are maximizing our talents and abilities *for the purpose* of contributing to the world around us. We feel fulfilled when we are giving the best of who we are to those around us. Contribution makes us happier individuals.

As Tony Robbins says, "The secret to happiness is giving."

This Book is for You if...

This book is for the woman who has abandoned her dreams and silenced the deepest desires of her heart.

This book is for the woman who might have given up hope that she can still rewrite her story.

This book is for those who have achieved fame, fortune, the corner office, popularity, and a massive social following.

It is also for those who have chosen to be teachers, mothers, nurses, lawyers, therapists, janitors, small business owners, artists, construction workers, interior designers, policewomen, accountants, or soldiers—no matter what profession you have chosen for yourself, this book is for you.

This book is not just about you redefining your success, apart from how our world has defined success for women; it is also your path to greater freedom.

This is your life and you get to decide what fulfills you. This book will show you HOW.

This book is for the woman who is ready to rebuild culture, one woman's worth at a time.

This book is for any woman who wants to be part of a movement fighting for women's fulfillment, including her own. It is about empowering every woman, but more importantly, equipping her with the mindset and skill set she needs to feel successful, and not just look successful.

This is not your typical book.

This book about "success" is actually a book about your personal fulfillment because that is what will make you feel truly successful. This book will give you a blueprint to become a fulfilled woman.

By the end of this book, you will have a proven formula to redesign every part of your life in order to have more life in your life. I will teach you how to use our 'Fulfillment Formula,' the same one that thousands of women are using across forty countries to redefine their own success.

This book will take you on a unique journey to rediscovering yourself again. This book is about how you want to live your life.

This is about growing in deeper fulfillment and becoming who you were fashioned to be. This book is about fulfilling your divine purpose.

This book is about bringing more life into your life.

This book is about hope, hope that you get to rewrite your own story and contribute to rewriting our collective stories as women.

This is about you inspiring other women to fulfill their dreams and hopes for their future.

The fact of life is that we all have an expiration date. We are each walking toward our grave, whether we think about it or not. We can use a serum to hold the fort down, but all roads lead to us growing older than we were yesterday.

This is ultimately a book about leaving your legacy, a legacy that will last long after you are gone.

Read and ponder. Take the time to allow the concepts of this book to penetrate the deepest parts of your heart.

We are not stuck when *fulfillment* becomes the metric in every season.

At the end of this book, you will have a path to success that is rooted in fulfillment.

This Book is Your Blueprint to Redefining Your Success as a Woman

As we journey through the rest of the book, you will begin to answer what success means for you. It will give you a deeper understanding of why you deserve success and the path to success has everything to do with what fulfills you. Your ability to redefine your success now and in the future will determine the quality of the rest of your life.

It is about discovering and developing the deepest desires of your heart. This is about you becoming who you were created to be—a fulfilled woman. Fulfilled because you have accomplished your purpose.

You were created to live a fulfilling and meaningful life, a life that makes you feel fully alive, so full of life that it inspires all those around you. To inspire means to breathe life. You will become the light that the world needs now.

As one of my favorite mentors would say, "The problem of darkness is not the darkness, it is the lack of light." You are called to become a light amongst the wounded hearts.

Your fulfillment can become the light with which you fill the hearts of those around you. When your life is full, it overflows, and you can fill everyone else's cup.

By redefining success to include fulfillment, we give every woman a chance at being the light she was created to be.

This book will show you how.
If you do the work, you will see miracles in your own life.

This is your "how to be fulfilled" book.
The rest of these pages will be a journey toward discovering a whole version of you.

P_{AUSE}

P_{ONDER}

A_{CT}

Chapter 1

1. What fulfills you as a woman?
2. What are some of the roadblocks to your fulfillment?
3. How have the Poisonous P's impacted your life?

CHAPTER 2

SUCCESS BEGINS WITH KNOWING WHAT YOU WANT

1. Success Cannot Be Apart From What You Want
2. What Do You Not Want to Put Up With Anymore?
3. The Wholeness Arena
4. Roadblocks to Getting What You Want
5. Consequences of Ignoring or Indulging in What you Want
6. The 10 Universal Desires that Unite Women
7. The Purpose of Focusing on What You Want

Success Cannot Be Apart From What You Want

Success begins with knowing what you want and don't want.

We have been told all our lives what a successful woman should look like, and these ideas are deeply ingrained in our minds. So ingrained, that the idea that success should begin with discovering what we want almost seems foreign and irrelevant.

Success tends to be divorced from our deepest desires. To some degree, it makes us feel that what we want does not matter. We base "success" on what our culture reveres as successful (the Poisonous P's) instead of what we actually want for ourselves.

The problem we are facing is that we empower women to pursue success based on what the culture has dictated makes a woman successful: power, prestige, popularity, possession, and perfection—instead of what fulfills her.

But before you ask what would make you successful, you first have to discover what you want in every part of your life.

Why? Because every part of you matters. And not only that. Every part of you impacts the other parts of you.

If you are having a difficult month at work, chances are your children, spouse, or friends can feel your frustrations. You can't pretend that you can compartmentalize yourself. You are an integrated human.

You can't expect a draining marriage not to impact your ability to work or care for your family. A stressful work environment has a ripple impact on your mental, emotional, physical, and spiritual health.

I want to shine a light on some myths surrounding "success."

- Success is not what your parents think you should want.
- Success is not what your husband thinks you should want.
- Success is not what your friends have decided for you.
- Success is not a metric of what the world thinks you should achieve.

The journey of discovering what you want is part of honoring yourself. It is taking into consideration that what you want matters—because you matter.

So many women ignore what they want because deep down inside, they do not believe they matter. They don't feel good enough and they question if they deserve to pursue what they want.

This is the guiding principle: Success begins with discovering what you want and don't want in every part of your life. It is about discovering the deepest desires of your heart.

A desire can act as a compass, guiding those who follow it.

Our deep desires are like the North Star; they become a compass on our life journey. They tell us where to cast our vision. These desires are a catalyst to aid us in discovering the things that matter most and reveal a big part of who we are.

After training thousands of women over the last two decades, I have learned that asking women what they want makes them feel very uncomfortable. It catches them off guard.

Most of the time, women have not taken the time to process the deepest desires of their hearts. Or, they have accepted the limiting belief that what they want is irrelevant to their success.

Why have we accepted that success is divorced from what we want? How can we be fulfilled unless it is rooted in the deepest desires of our hearts?

No wonder so many of us feel unfulfilled. We have not laid the necessary foundation to create a fulfilling life: the foundation of knowing what we want and don't want.

It is time we change the narrative of what success means for women. To be a successful woman, you have to begin by knowing what you want in your life. It is an essential first step to redefining success for you.

If you want a life that fulfills you, then every part of your life must be full of life. It is about creating a life of wholeness, meaning every part of you feels fully alive.

What you want is vital to your fulfillment. Success therefore cannot be separated from the life you want.

If you are going to pursue success that fulfills you, you first need to know what makes your heart fulfilled. What brings you joy, peace, and happiness?

"Wholeness," as we define it in The Woman School, means being fully alive and growing in harmony with your original design. Original design means that you are in alignment with your unique purpose.

Wholeness is about honoring every part of you. It is a way for you to validate that you are not just parts of yourself, you are a whole woman. Wholeness requires you to intentionally design every part of your life so you can decide what brings you joy. No one can do that for you.

Consider these questions:

- Who do I want to be?
- How would I describe my mental and emotional health? Can these areas be better?
- How would I describe my physical and spiritual life? Can these areas be better?
- What do I want from my friendships?
- How do I want to feel in my intimate relationships?
- What kind of work fulfills me?
- How would I like my home and family life to feel?
- How would I describe my wealth? Do I want something different?

What Do You Not Want to Put Up With Anymore?

I remember listening to Tony Robbins. He asked, "What pain do you not want to put up with in your life anymore?"

It was a very powerful question that I had never considered before.

I quickly wrote my list:

- I was tired of not having help and doing everything on my own, which made me impatient with my children.
- I was tired of not having enough money to support my dreams for our family. To be more specific, I wanted to take my children to the Philippines, so I could share with them where I grew up. I wanted them to get a first-hand experience of the poverty in the Philippines that taught me so much.
- I did not want to put up with not having enough resources to educate my children.
- I didn't want to settle for reaching thousands of women instead of millions—simply because I didn't know how to build a business.

The exercise of writing out what I no longer wanted to put up with gave me language for my struggle. I didn't realize that so much of my struggle was because I just tolerated what I didn't want, instead of finding a solution to get what I wanted.

I think most women would agree that we are quick to accept the life that we don't want instead of designing a life that could get us what we want. Most of us just settle because we don't believe we have a choice.

I am here to tell you that you have a choice.

And it begins with identifying what you want and don't want.

Sometimes, the quickest way to figure out what you want is to identify what you don't want. So, now it's your turn.

Question #1: "What are the things I do not want to put up with anymore?"

Perhaps...

- You don't want to put up with being taken for granted by your man.
- You don't want to continue your long commute to work or be in a toxic workplace.
- You don't want to come home to chaos where your home and children are a mess.
- You don't want to put up with not having enough money to pay for family vacations.
- You don't want to remain operating with low energy or be in a constant state of overwhelm.
- You don't want to put up with feeling restless and not knowing what to do with your life.
- You don't want to continue dealing with a mother-in-law who criticizes you.
- You want to stop feeling like a failure.

Question #2: "Why am I putting up with what I don't want?"

- Do I feel stuck?
- Do I believe there is no way out of my misery?
- Do I feel like this is as good as it will ever get?
- Do I feel like there is an ingrained belief that getting what I want is bad?
- What are other limiting beliefs that are holding me back from actually thinking about what I want?

Even the permission to think about what you want could feel sinful to some women.

Why? Because what you wanted was never an option growing up. No one asked what you wanted, and you didn't feel like your opinion mattered.

You are not alone if you feel a level of resistance when you start to talk about what you want and don't want. You resist because you've been told that what you want is bad, not valid, or that it doesn't matter.

How do you know that you matter?
When your desires are validated, you feel like you matter.

If you grew up in a family where you were ridiculed for what you wanted, then maybe you buried the desires of your heart because that is what was needed to survive your family culture.

But that was then. You don't have to be silenced anymore.
You can give yourself permission to go back to that little girl inside of you and ask her...what does she really really want?

When we ask ourselves what we don't want, we can give ourselves permission to face parts of our life that we might not be aware are creating a negative ripple effect in the other parts of us. Knowing what we don't want is an important step to acknowledging the parts of us that we have ignored or disregarded as unimportant.

I want to invite you to see your life with eyes of wholeness, beginning with the wholeness arena. The exercise below is just the beginning of a journey to designing every part of your life.

I created very specific questions that you can use to ponder each part of your arena. The goal for these questions is to dig a little deeper and start to unearth what you want and don't want.

What we are doing here is bringing a deeper awareness of the current state of each part of your arena. This is a digging exercise and if at any point the questions sting a little, please pause for a moment and be gentle with yourself. For now, wrestle with some of the questions and allow them to penetrate your heart.

Happy digging.

The Wholeness Arena

Introducing the Wholeness Arena.

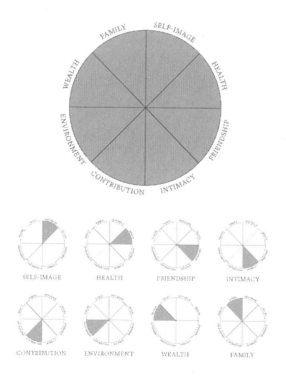

Figure 2.1

WHOLENESS ARENA

Go to redefinesuccessforwomen.com for a free printable download.

Each part of the wholeness arena represents a facet of a woman's life that is very important. These parts are equally divided to represent the equal importance of each part.

Here are the eight parts to the Wholeness Arena:

1. Self-Image
2. Health
3. Friendship
4. Intimacy
5. Contribution
6. Environment
7. Wealth
8. Family

Wholeness means that we feel whole because each of these parts of our life has been intentionally fulfilled, meaning we feel happy and alive. To live a life of wholeness requires us to be intentional about how we want each part of our life to "feel."

If nothing was holding you back, how do you want each part of your life to be?

What you want cannot happen by default, it can only happen by design.

Wholeness means complete. It doesn't mean perfect.

It means that regardless of the circumstances in each part of your arena, you are choosing to see the good while simultaneously creating strategic solutions to achieve what you want.

It is living with gratitude in the present while casting a vision of a hopeful future.

It is a profound understanding that the present moment is a gift and that our future is our responsibility.

Wholeness is not an arrival, it is a way of life. A life where we are intentional about nourishing every part of us so we can give from a full cup.

Seeing with eyes of wholeness will help us stay vigilant against giving from an empty cup.

Let me give you a backstory on why we started calling this the Wholeness Arena. I was inspired to create it after reading Theodore Roosevelt's 1910 speech, "The Man in the Arena."

"It is not the critic who counts; not the man who points out how the strong man stumbles, or where the doer of deeds could have done them better. The credit belongs to the man who is actually in the arena, whose face is marred by dust and sweat and blood; who strives valiantly; who errs, who comes short again and again, because there is no effort without error and shortcoming; but who does actually strive to do the deeds; who knows great enthusiasms, the great devotions; who spends himself in a worthy cause; who at the best knows, in the end, the triumph of high achievement, and who at the worst, if he fails, at least fails while daring greatly, so that his place shall never be with those cold and timid souls who neither know victory nor defeat."

His words were a significant inspiration to me because as a business owner and a mom of eight, I have to fight to keep every part of my arena fully alive. I can't just achieve my business goals at the expense of losing my ability to be the mom, wife, and friend that I want to be. I have to be very strategic about intentionally designing and acquiring new strategies to help me achieve a life of wholeness.

I work hard day in and out to build new skills so that I can take care of every part of my life.

The more skills I acquire, the easier it is to integrate every part of my life. The more discipline I have, the smoother life is.

Discipline and hard work are the prices I pay for a life of wholeness.

Discipline is hard. Sometimes it takes blood, sweat, and tears, but it is worth the price.

When I ponder Roosevelt's words, I think about the battle that is required to fight in the arena of your life. You have to really fight for the life you want.

To have what you want in every part of your arena means that you have to endure the hard work necessary to achieve the life you want for yourself. You can have what you want as long as you are willing to discipline yourself to achieve it.

The alternative would be to sit on the sidelines of your life and never fight for what you want.

The woman in the arena is a woman who strategically designs every part of her life based on what fulfills her. She ultimately takes responsibility for her life of wholeness.

I want to invite you to consider a life of wholeness by first identifying what you want and don't want in every part of your life. I will be going deeper into these concepts in the next few chapters.

For now, look over the brief descriptions and begin to describe the circumstances of each part of your arena. Ponder what you want and don't want, giving yourself permission to explore the desires of your heart.

As we continue to journey together, we are going to bring greater clarity to these desires. For now, just explore your own heart.

Figure 2.2

WHOLENESS ARENA

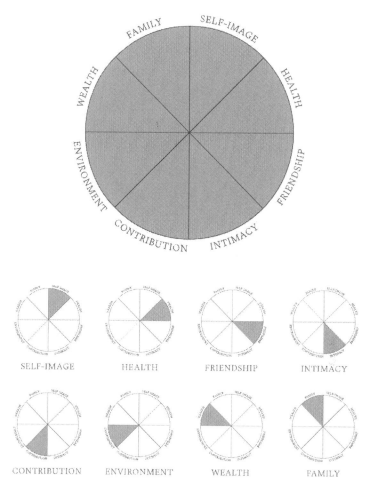

Go to redefinesuccessforwomen.com for a free printable download.

Self-Image: Your self-image is the opinion you hold of yourself. Right now, you have a set of beliefs and opinions about yourself that you have come to believe as true. These beliefs you carry with you either help or harm you.

The goal is for you to design a self-image that is in harmony with the woman you are choosing to become. The opinion that you hold of yourself sets the foundation of how you make decisions about your life.

Figure 2.3

SELF-IMAGE

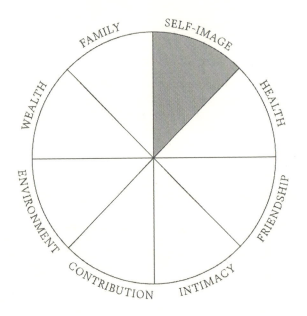

Questions to Ponder:

1. How would I describe my current self-image?
2. Is my opinion of myself positive or negative?
3. How did I develop my self-image?
4. What self-image would I want to acquire for myself?
5. Am I satisfied or unsatisfied with my current self-image? Why?

Health: We describe health as an integration of our mental, emotional, physical, and spiritual health. Our health impacts every part of the arena, so being intentional about how we manage our minds, command our emotions, take care of our bodies, and deepen spiritual growth is vital to be fulfilled in this part of our arena.

The goal is optimal health. The purpose of optimal health is to maximize your potential and be fully alive.

Figure 2.4

HEALTH

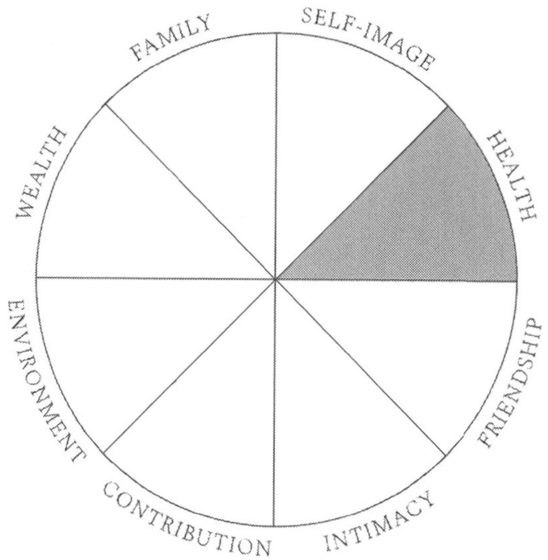

Questions to Ponder:

1. How would I describe my current mental and emotional health?
2. How are my mental and emotional health impacting the other parts of my arena?

3. How would I describe my physical health?
4. Am I taking responsibility for taking care of my body?
5. How would I describe my spiritual health?

Friendship: Friendships are designed to help us along the journey of fulfilling our purpose. They accompany us through the different seasons of life. The purpose of friendship is to help us stay on track so we can continue to grow in harmony with who we were created to be.

The goal of friendship is to nourish you along the journey while also holding you accountable to becoming your highest and best self.

Figure 2.5

FRIENDSHIP

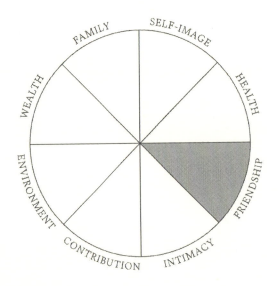

Questions to Ponder:

1. Describe my current friendships.
2. Are my friends helping me become the best version of myself?

3. Have some of my friendships (current or previous) become toxic? Why?
4. How would I want to improve my current friendships?
5. Do my friends hold me accountable?

Intimacy: Intimacy is sharing the most sacred part of our life with someone who has earned the right to be there. It is a vulnerable space where we let our guard down and reveal a big part of who we are. Intimacy with another person requires us to grow in deeper self-awareness in our personal relationship with ourselves.

The goal for intimacy is to cultivate a relationship with someone who honors your unconditional worth and sees your unique and irreplaceable purpose in their life. You cannot squander the most sacred parts of yourself, so finding the right person is a critical decision.

Figure 2.6

INTIMACY

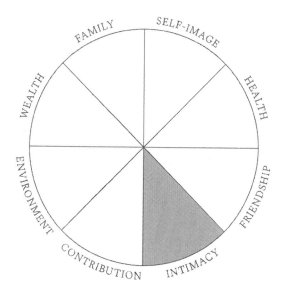

Questions to Ponder:

1. Does the person I have allowed into the most sacred areas of my life honor my unconditional worth and make me feel special?
2. Whether I am in a relationship or not, do I feel prepared to be in a healthy and wholesome relationship? Why or why not?
3. What are some old wounds that might be holding me back from opening my heart fully?
4. Do I value and respect myself enough to hold people accountable for treating me with respect? Why or why not?
5. Do I put up with a relationship where I am constantly being criticized? Why?

Contribution: Every woman is born with a desire and a responsibility to contribute something meaningful with her life. Our contribution is an extension of who we are. This could be our work, service to the community, or our contribution in our homes.

The goal of contribution is to design a life where you can become a constant light to those around you. A life of contribution is an intentional life, made up of both giving and receiving.

Ultimately, it is not what you do, but who you are that becomes your greatest contribution.

Figure 2.7

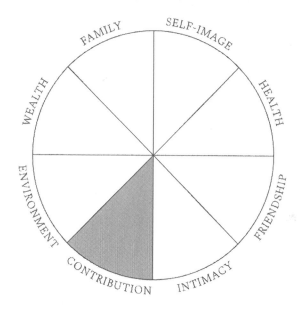

Questions to Ponder:

1. Am I currently doing work that inspires me and gives me life? Why or why not?
2. Do I feel like I am maximizing my full potential? Why or why not?
3. Am I currently in a toxic working environment where I don't feel valued? Why? What is keeping me there?
4. What is holding me back from finding work that I love?
5. How would I describe my contribution at home?

Environment: Our environment is twofold, composed of the space and the people we choose to be surrounded by. Our external environment impacts our interior environment (our thoughts and feelings). We have to do our part to take responsibility in creating a space for growth, peace, and creativity.

The goal is to cultivate a beautiful environment that inspires light.

Figure 2.8

ENVIRONMENT

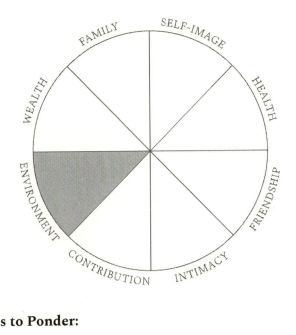

Questions to Ponder:

1. Describe my current environment.
2. Does my current environment inspire me and give me peace? Why or why not?
3. How is my current environment impacting the different parts of my arena?
4. What is the most challenging part of my current environment? What is the best part?
5. What do I no longer want to put up with in my current environment (home or work)? Why?

Wealth: Wealth is an abundance of time, treasure, and talent for the purpose of contribution. It is first and foremost a mindset of both gratitude and generosity, as well as a mindset of abundance from which we have the freedom to give freely. It is having the ability to possess wealth while being detached from it, because it is not what we have that fulfills us, it is what we do with what we have that determines the quality of our fulfillment.

The goal for your wealth is to design a life in which you feel there is always more than enough, regardless of how much you have.

Figure 2.9

WEALTH

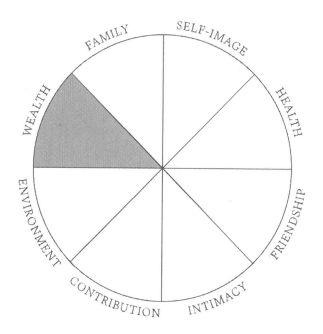

Ponder these questions:

1. Do I currently have an abundance or scarcity mindset? Explain.
2. How is my current understanding of wealth impacting every part of my arena?
3. What do I wish you had more of: time, treasure, talent, or all of them? Why?
4. What is holding me back from creating true wealth? Why?
5. Has wealth been a challenging part of my arena? Why or why not?

Family: The family is the foundation that establishes the core of who you are. It is designed to be a place of growth and nourishment. How you show up to your family can either be a source of significant generational contribution, or significant generational trauma.

The goal is to create a family life that brings you life, not robs you of it.

Figure 2.10

FAMILY

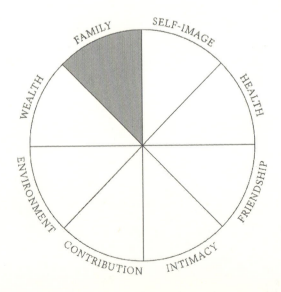

Ponder these questions:

1. How would I describe my current family situation?
2. How would I describe my family of origin? Was it positive or negative?
3. What are some of the wounds that I have endured from my parents?
4. Have I taken the time to heal from old wounds? How is this impacting me, positively or negatively?
5. What pain have I inherited from my family of origin that is now being transferred to my current family unit?

As you assess these parts of your own life, the goal is self-awareness. From there, you can determine what you want and don't want in every area of the arena. You no longer have to be a victim of a life you don't want.

It is hard to overemphasize the importance of knowing what you want in every part of your life. It is time to begin the journey of ownership in your life of wholeness.

Roadblocks to Getting What You Want

There will always be roadblocks to achieving what we want. The goal is to find new tools to overcome these roadblocks.

We can't just sit still and do nothing, and succumb to the belief that we don't have a choice. We have to shatter any limiting beliefs we hold about what is possible.

Let's identify some of the roadblocks that might be keeping you from getting what you want. By identifying the roadblocks, you give yourself a better chance at designing a life of wholeness.

Roadblock #1: Not Knowing What You Want

You don't know how to discover what you want and don't want. That is probably the norm.

If you grew up in the "because I said so" generation, then you were programmed to believe that what you wanted was irrelevant. You would have also been programmed to ignore what you wanted.

Yet, observing what you want and don't want is a mental muscle that must be used in order for you to get stronger. If you were trained to ignore what you want, then there is a chance that that muscle has begun to atrophy.

So, how do you begin to use that muscle? You begin by using it imperfectly. It's like going to the gym and feeling incompetent because you don't know how to use the equipment. At first, your muscles feel like mush. You might feel insecure because you can't even carry a five-pound weight.

But eventually, just by using your muscles, it gets easier. And if you are consistent, you will be lifting fifty pounds in no time.

It is the same idea as developing your ability to identify what you want and don't want. This is a muscle that needs to be continually developed.

To continue with this exercise, access the worksheet (free download), "What You Want and Don't Want," at redefinesuccessforwomen.com. Here, write down what you want and don't want in every part of your arena.

Writing is key. Just braindump.
Writing helps you wire your brain.

By writing, you declutter the jumble of thoughts in your mind and unload that burden onto paper. It will help bring clarity to what you want and don't.

I designed this worksheet in this way so that you get to see on one page how every part impacts the other. It was created intentionally to help you begin to see with eyes of wholeness. This one page gives you evidence of how integrated you are.

Figure 2.11

WANT AND DON'T WANT

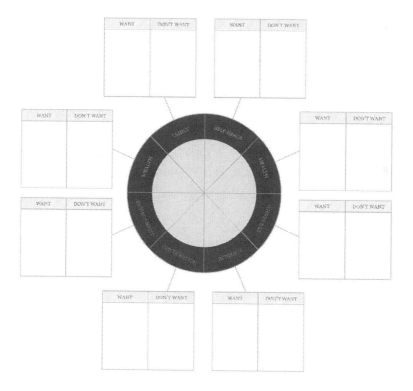

Go to redefinesuccessforwomen.com for a free printable download.

As you fill out this worksheet, here are some guidelines to remember:

1. Don't hold back.
    a. Be careful not to judge your thoughts before you can process them. Simply write and get it out of your system. Be brutally honest. Do not edit or censor yourself.
    b. You don't have to share this with anyone (unless you want to), but the point is that you don't hold back.
2. It might hurt.
    a. But this is part of the process. Think deep, cry tears of regret, but get it all out. Emotions come when you realize you have silenced what you wanted for years. If you need to pause, you can.
    b. Finally giving yourself permission to identify what you want and don't want could potentially unearth old wounds. This may reveal where you need some healing, so don't be afraid to be honest—even if it hurts. Get the necessary help if you need to.
3. It might take time.
    a. If this has been a dormant muscle, it will take time to awaken it. Be patient and kind with yourself. This exercise seems simple, but if the muscle is weak, it will take time.
    b. Don't give up, be gentle with yourself, and find the courage to face yourself.
    c. Find a mentor if you need to.
4. Notice how every part impacts the other.
    a. For example, pay attention to how your self-image impacts your health, your intimacy, or your environment.
    b. This process is an awakening process, learning to see with eyes of wholeness.

5. Make time for this.
    a. Find a quiet place where you will have time and space to think and ponder. Journal if you need to. Take this book and retreat away for a few hours. It will be a gift to yourself.
    b. Give yourself the freedom to ask difficult questions.

Roadblock #2: Fear of Failure

Fear holds us back from pursuing the things that we want to pursue.
Fear of failure.
Fear of disappointing the people we love.
Fear of critics.
Fear of what others might think.
Fear of not being good enough.

Fear can cripple a woman, keeping her from pursuing the deepest desires of her heart.

Everyone fails, yet most of us are afraid of failing.

Fear is part of the human experience, but how we choose to face our fears determines what we allow ourselves to achieve.

Fear can be conditioned. If we grew up in a fear-based home, we might be risk averse, which could hold us back from taking a leap into our dreams.

Clarifying what we want and don't want might trigger deep fears of not being able to achieve what we want.

Fear is normal.

Fear could even be healthy to some degree because it keeps us alive. But staying in a constant state of fear is abnormal; that is not healthy.

What we need to do is to manage our fears and not be a slave to them. We can do this by reshaping and forming our perception of the fear we are experiencing.

When thoughts of fear arise, pay attention to whether or not there is any real danger. If the fear you are ruminating on is only in your thoughts, you can use scripts to replace your negative thoughts.

At The Woman School, we use scripts to neurologically rewire our brains so we can expand our mindset. We have thousands of scripts to help train women so they can replace negative thoughts that no longer serve them.

Here is a script you can use every time you feel fear of failing. You can add, subtract, or find a script that suits you best.

"I fail forward fast and learn from it."

If you can learn to shift your perception of failure to an experience to harvest from, then you can give yourself permission to pursue what you really want, even at the risk of failing.

Roadblock #3: Lack of Role Models

Who are role models for you? Where are the women who are intentionally designing a life of wholeness? Women who are fulfilled in every part of their life?

When I was designing a life of wholeness, my mentor told me to search for a couple who had a beautiful marriage. I had seen such pain in my parents' marriage that I didn't even know what a beautiful marriage could look like. I needed a role model to break some of my limiting beliefs surrounding marriage.

I found them, and they changed my life forever.

Ate Deeda was a 5' Filipino lady married to a 6'4" Irish man who spoke fluent Filipino. They were madly in love with each other. It was fascinating to watch how much he loved her; I can still see the way he would look at her, he was in awe of her. He even wrote love notes! And more importantly, I saw the eyes of a woman who felt admired by her man. Wow! I had never seen anything like it.

Their example broke through what was possible in my mind. It was like realizing that the world was round and not actually flat. Yes, it was earth-shattering.

I was so fascinated by how they loved each other, that I asked to study them. And because they were so gracious, they let me. I studied their relationship like a hawk because, for the first time, I saw what I wanted.

I spent a whole decade studying couples and relationships before I met my Ryan. I cannot emphasize enough what a massive impact these role models had in shaping my decisions regarding marriage. And not only that, they became the blueprint by which I designed who I wanted to spend the rest of my life with.

Role models give us hope for what is possible. They help us shatter our own limiting beliefs.

Your task is to find three role models in your life right now who can help you see what is possible.

Using the template below, "Discover Your Role Models," identify and study role models for every part of your life.

When looking for your role models, consider the women you know personally, women you respect, those you follow on social media, authors, speakers, and friends.

Fill in these sections:

WHO—Who is my role model in this arena? Name her.
WHY—Why do I admire her?
HOW—How can I learn from her and implement these lessons in my life?

Figure 2.12

DISCOVER YOUR ROLE MODELS

WHAT	WHO	WHY	HOW
Self-Image			
Mental and Emotional Health			
Physical and Spiritual Health			
Friendship			
Intimacy			
Contribution			
Environment			
Wealth			
Family			

Go to redefinesuccessforwomen.com for a free printable download.

Caveat: It would be hard to find the same role model for every arena. You might have a role model for health or wealth and a different role model for intimacy or family life. That is okay. Finding someone who has everything you want is not typical.

After you complete this worksheet, consider the following:

- Was it easy to find role models?
- What were some of the challenges?

Roadblock #4: Stress

Stress hijacks the mind, rendering it incapable of thinking freely about the things you want.

Stress feels like you are being chased by a lion—all day, every day. If you are being chased by a lion, that is not the time to ponder what you want and don't want in life—it is time to run!

The stresses of life do not look like lions, but they can cause the same anxiety and panic. Maybe your "lion" is a horrible marriage, a job you hate, a chaotic home, sick children, or financial problems.

Think for a moment about how our world has dramatically shifted. It is faster, louder, and busier.

Faster means there is no time to pause and recalibrate. We quickly move from one thing to another, without rejuvenating ourselves.

Our world is louder, meaning there are nearly constant external distractions that inhibit us from thinking about our interior life. Social media, text messaging, movies, news, and the internet are loud distractions, keeping us from focusing on what matters.

The world is busier. The internet allows us to be constantly available, and the options of where to spend our time are endless. We don't run out of things to busy our minds and our bodies. If we do not know how to say no, then it is easy to be overwhelmed, and that leads to stress.

The major culprit to stress is that we lack the training to manage our minds. We can't control the external noises around us, but the more skills we develop, the more we can tune out the distractions.

I wish I could snap my finger and teach you how to manage your stress, but it doesn't work that way. If you want to become a gymnast, you can't just read about it—you have to *train-up* for it.

So, how do we take away stress as a roadblock?

If you want to learn how to manage stress so it does not inhibit you from living the life you want, then you have to invest in training your mind and developing your skill set. This is called mind management.

We have to train. We must train our minds and build new skills. We have to learn how to manage our thoughts against distractions and build new skills that protect us and help us to focus.

Consequences of Ignoring or Indulging in What you Want

I was coaching a woman in her 70s. Together we went through the arena, and I asked her what she wanted in each area. Her tears just kept falling. In a tender voice, she replied, "I've never really asked myself what I wanted."

She was a great mother. She took care of the people she loved. She worked diligently for years in the same company. But the idea of

asking herself what she wanted never crossed her heart. She lived her life doing what she thought everyone else wanted.
The tears that fell during our coaching call were tears of regret because she had never considered what she wanted.

How can we expect a woman to feel fulfilled if she was never able to make a conscious and deliberate effort to discover and develop the desires of her heart?

By ignoring what she wants, she also ignores what is possible in her life.

This gets complicated, because how we discover our purpose is by discovering what moves our soul.

But when we ignore what we want, we might miss the very purpose for which we were fashioned.

When we ignore what we want, we risk anger, resentment, and anxiety.

Ignoring what we want also has negative consequences on those around us.

The ache of regret and resentment burdens many women who have given so much to those around them. They feel an emptiness inside because parts of them have died. They can become resentful and bitter.

I have this hunch, and it is only a hunch—I have no data to back it up quite yet—but based on my twenty years of having a front-row seat to women's pain, I suspect that midlife crises come from ignoring the deepest desires of our hearts every step of the way. When we feel stifled, eventually there becomes a strong need to break free from the cage.

We can no longer allow women to ignore their desires if we are to create a culture of women who feel alive.

The same is true for indulging in what we want.
Indulging in what we want has similar effects.

You can't eat whatever you want and expect to be healthy. Eventually, these harmful choices will catch up with you.

You can't endlessly binge on Netflix shows any time you want, and expect to accomplish your goals in life.

We refer to indulging as the "whatever you want" model, and it does not work.

Just because we are free to do whatever we want, it does not mean we should.

To be fulfilled means we have to order what we want to be in harmony with our highest good.

There is an idea in the coaching world that it is up to the client to do whatever they want in order to be happy. I just disagree.

Because what we want might not be our highest good.

I am Filipino and I love white rice. But because my family has pre-diabetic tendencies, I cannot eat rice every day, even though I want to.

Indulging in the "whatever I want" model will not lead to me the fulfillment I deeply crave.

Simply chasing what we want might not be our best path to fulfillment. Making the best choices for the life we really want requires maturity.

The goal of discovering what you want in every arena of your life is to observe what you want, while simultaneously learning what fulfills you. It develops self-awareness.

This book is about self-awareness and we are just getting started.

The 10 Universal Desires that Unite Women

Let me introduce you to the universal desire.

What is it that women crave?

There is so much division happening in the political sphere, in our immediate families, and in the social media world, that it is hard to imagine what could unite us as women.

But, we have much more in common than we think.

Our Universal Desires as women unite us.

What are Universal Desires?

Universal Desires are the deepest longings etched in every woman's heart. They are universal because they are part of the human condition.
These Universal Desires reveal to us what fulfills us.

Our goal is to mature our current desires to grow in harmony with what fulfills us. We want to align what we want with what is best for us.
We know that the "whatever you want" model does not always work if it is not in harmony with our highest good.

These Universal Desires hold us accountable to pursuing our highest and best self.

There are ten Universal Desires that unite us as women. Because we are all uniquely created, what we want is unique to each of us. What each woman wants will look different, but how we want to feel is the same. At our core, we share the same human need for fulfillment. For example, you could want to be a doctor, teacher, stay-at-home mom, or astronaut; our paths are different but we all share a desire to be fulfilled regardless of our profession.

These Universal Desires are written on every heart, regardless of what season of life we are in.

I outline these Universal Desires as your guide as you make decisions on how you want to design a life of wholeness, a life that ultimately brings greater fulfillment.

I want you to ponder each one and discover what it means for you. These Universal Desires allow us to focus on what unites us as women, instead of what divides us.

As I begin to briefly share each one, take the time to wrestle with them and give yourself permission to question your own beliefs about what is possible in your life.

REDEFINE SUCCESS FOR WOMEN

Ten Universal Desires of Women

Figure 2.13

10 UNIVERSAL DESIRES

1. CONFIDENCE
2. FREEDOM
3. PEACE OF MIND
4. OPTIMAL HEALTH
5. FULFILLMENT
6. MEANING AND PURPOSE
7. MEANINGFUL WORK
8. TO LOVE AND BE LOVED
9. ORDER
10. ABUNDANCE

Go to redefinesuccessforwomen.com for a free printable download.

These ten core universal desires go beyond culture, age, or season of life. They apply to every woman, everywhere.

The purpose of clarifying these Universal Desires is to learn to choose our highest good, because our highest good is what ultimately fulfills us. In this way, we will be able to redefine success for ourselves.

As you read through these descriptions, think about how each one fits into your life right now. Rate yourself 0-10. "0" means you have never considered this desire for yourself. "10" means you have incorporated this universal desire in the design for your life.

#1 Confidence
Are you confident in who you are? Rate yourself 0-10.

A confident woman is free to show up fully as herself. Confidence is not just looking the part—it is believing in yourself. It is not merely external.

There is a Universal Desire to be confident because ultimately, we each have a deep desire to be accepted. What we want is the capacity to be valued as we are, with no need to pretend or prove ourselves.

Confident women are attractive because they exude freedom, the freedom to be who they are, and they are accepted. This is what we universally desire.

We are not born confident. We become confident through competence. Competence means we have developed the mindset and skill sets we need to be competent in a specific skill.

For example, a confident speaker is confident because she has built the mindset and skills that allow her to be a confident speaker.
She built confidence through competence, which meant she had to train for it.

In The Woman School, we give women a formula for confidence. We believe that every woman can become confident as long as she is willing to *train-up* for it. Our confidence formula is about building compounding skills so your confidence is not fleeting or external—it comes from within.

When you are skilled in routine, boundaries, and managing your mind, your confidence improves. When you learn how to communicate effectively and learn how to show up in a room, you will see your confidence grow.

Confidence is simply a learned skill. Training is the key ingredient to true self-confidence.

The Universal Desire for confidence is what our hearts crave.

#2 Freedom
Are you free to choose your highest good? Rate yourself 0-10.

The Universal Desire for freedom is strong. No woman wants to be in chains. However, external freedoms, such as the freedom to vote, to work, or to own property, are not the freedoms I am speaking about here, though these are obviously freedoms all women deserve.

The freedom I am speaking of is the freedom to choose our highest good.

You don't say to yourself, "I choose mediocrity!" No, of course not. But you do choose to spend hours scrolling through social media because you have not developed the will to choose your highest good.

To be free means that I have the resilience, the capacity, and the will to choose what is best for me, regardless of how I feel. For example, "I choose to exercise even though I don't feel like working out."

When we are free to choose our highest good, we can design a life that fulfills us. We do not have to be slaves to what everyone else thinks we should do with our lives. We are free to choose what we believe is our highest good.

#3 Peace of Mind
Do you experience constant peace of mind? Rate yourself 0-10.

Who doesn't want peace of mind? No one volunteers for chaos, stress, anxiety, and overwhelm. Peace of mind hinges on knowing how to manage your mind.

Peace of mind is something that our hearts long for. We ache for it. Regardless of what we want to do with our lives, we each share a Universal Desire for peace of mind.

Peace of mind is not achieved by "perfection" of our external circumstances, but rather by our ability to choose how we perceive our external circumstances. It requires us to train our minds and be vigilant against what robs us of peace.

We want to be strong and resilient against the uncertain external circumstances that are inevitable. We don't want to live our lives as victims of everything that happens around us.

#4 Optimal Health
Are you mentally, emotionally, physically, and spiritually strong? Rate yourself 0-10.

Every person wants a healthy mind, body, and spirit.

We don't want to be tired. We want to have abundant energy to pursue the dreams that we hold in our hearts.

We deeply want to operate at our maximum energy level and not waste our time, treasure, or talent waiting for life to pass us by. We share a Universal Desire to maximize our full potential.

#5 Fulfillment
Are you fulfilled? Rate yourself 0-10.

What does it mean to be fulfilled? It means that we are fully alive in every part of our life.

This applies not only to our marriages. Not only to our family or home. Not only to our careers. It applies to every aspect of the arena.

Fulfillment will come when every part of your life is intentionally designed, based on what you want, in harmony with the Universal Desire.

#6 Meaning and Purpose
Are you living with meaning and purpose? Rate yourself 0-10.

We have a Universal Desire to live with meaning and purpose. A life void of purpose and meaning burdens our souls. When we are born, we carry within us a commission that only we can fulfill. Our time on earth is meant to be spent developing the mindset and skill sets we need to fulfill that divine purpose.

Humans share a Universal Desire for meaning and purpose. We want to believe and we want to know that our existence and our time on earth matters. We want to know that our time is not wasted.

We share a Universal Desire to live life with a profound purpose that makes us feel alive.

#7 Meaningful Work
Is your work meaningful to you? Rate yourself 0-10.

Doing meaningful work gives us evidence of our value. Every woman is valuable, but not every woman believes in her value.

Doing meaningful work—work that contributes to the well-being of another—gives us evidence that our life matters.

We want work that brings more joy and meaning.

We all want to know that our contribution impacts others. Whether you are a working or stay-at-home mom, your work is meaningful.

#8 To Love and Be Loved
Are you free to love and be loved? Rate yourself 0-10.

We want to know that we are worthy of love; that we are capable of loving and being loved.

Yet women have endured so much pain because they were taught that they had to prove that they were lovable.

Proving ourselves over and over causes us to put up walls and harden our hearts.

We each have a universal desire to love deeply and be deeply loved. When a woman is fully loved and celebrated, she comes alive because she was made for love.

#9 Order
Is your life ordered well? Rate yourself 0-10.

Disorder and disorganization result in chaos—external and internal chaos. No one wants to live in chaos.

Our external environment impacts our interior environment and our peace of mind. Order within that environment reduces stress. It allows us to feel safe in our homes or workplace. What our hearts long for is a space that allows our mind, body, and spirit to rest.

Order is key to creating harmony in our homes, which can then spread to our communities, and our society.

In my house of eight children, it takes a lot of work to create healthy discipline to protect the harmony and joy in our home. But it is worth the work. When I see the joy and peace in our home (even though it is loud and we certainly have moments of chaos), I know this order is a result of intentional and dedicated work. My husband and I have worked hard to establish external order because we know how it can impact our children's peace of mind.

To achieve order does not mean that everything has to be perfect. It simply means that things are working together well, and your environment is contributing to the joy and freedom of the people who live there.

#10 Abundance
Do you live a life of abundance? Rate yourself 0-10.

We don't want to live in scarcity, skimping our way through every decision because we think there is not enough.

Abundance is a state of gratitude and generosity. It makes us feel alive.

If we knew how to create an abundant life, that is what we would choose: a life where there is more than enough to give: time, treasure, or talent. We want the ability to make choices not based on a lack, but rather on abundance.

Abundance gives us the freedom to choose.

Abundance allows us to expand who we are and our mission in the world. Abundance means we are willing to break the boundaries of what is possible in our life.

The Purpose of Focusing on What You Want

Most of us focus on what we don't want. Why do we do this? I think it is because we fear disappointment. We would rather plan for the worst-case scenario than feel the pain of disappointment.

We focus so intently on planning for the worst, that we don't even let ourselves imagine the best-case scenario. We assume it's not possible. Instead of focusing on what we want—we only see what we do not want.

If you are someone who has spent most of her life assuming the worst so that you didn't have to risk being disappointed, I want to invite you to be open to a new way of thinking.

I will give you scientific evidence of why it is important to instead focus on what you want.

Figure 2.14

Reticular Activating System

The *Reticular Activating System (RAS)* is a network of neurons located in the brain stem that filters information that is important to you.

Our brains are a survival mechanism. At any given moment, only a certain amount of information is actually useful to your brain, so it filters everything else out. The RAS helps you expand what you focus on.

For example, if you are looking for a white van, all of a sudden you are seeing white vans on the road that you didn't notice before, simply because you were not paying attention to them. They were always there, but you didn't notice them because you were not focused on them.

When we choose to focus on something specific, it helps us filter out other information so we can find what we are looking for. Essentially, our RAS is working to help us to see what we want to see.

Because of the power of the RAS, a problem can arise when we focus on what we don't want: we miss opportunities to achieve what we want.

By focusing on the worst-case scenario, we don't give the brain an option to look for the best-case scenario. And we often get exactly what we are looking for.

When I finally understood the RAS, this knowledge gave me enough evidence to change my own limiting belief: I had to stop focusing on what I didn't want, for fear of disappointment. It was far more beneficial to focus on what I wanted!

The RAS goes to work for us, based on what we focus on, thus providing scientific evidence that we may find what we want.

The purpose of focusing on what you want is to work with your brain to help you strategically achieve what you want.

When we focus on what we want, we take responsibility for designing every part of our life and we use our God-given brain to help us pursue the life we want.

Each time you feel doubtful about your life and you start to look at everything that is wrong, remind yourself of your RAS and shift your thoughts to focus on what you want. Awareness is key. You have to be hyper-aware when you are spiraling into thoughts of doubt, so you can pivot quickly.

If you need more evidence to focus on what you want, then I encourage you to study the *Reticular Activating System*. It will help you break free of your own limiting beliefs.

Now, finally, it is the time in this journey when we can connect the dots between success and having a dream.

P_{AUSE}
P_{ONDER}
A_{CT}

Chapter 2

1. What do you not want to put up with anymore?
2. What are some roadblocks to getting what you want?
3. How do the Universal Desires impact the way you see yourself right now?

CHAPTER 3

SUCCESS MUST BE ROOTED IN FULFILLMENT

---

1. The Old Model of Success Does Not Work
2. Why Do We Need to Redefine Success for Women?
3. The Purpose of a Successful Life
4. Guideposts to Redefining Success
5. The Fulfillment Formula
6. The New Model of Success is Rooted in Fulfillment
7. Unfulfilled People Become Toxic to Our Community
8. How to Begin to Design a Fulfilling Life

The Old Model of Success Does Not Work

Quick summary.

Chapter 1 was about the crisis and giving language to our internal struggle of being unfulfilled. We identified how the current toxic metric of success has poisoned the ability of women to feel valued. It is the realization that you are not alone. Chapter 1 is all about grace and mercy for yourself and seeing the war against women.

Chapter 2 gave us permission to discover the deepest desires of our hearts. We learned about the universal desire that unites women. Chapter 2 was also about understanding the importance of developing what we want to align with our highest good.

My goal for Chapter 1 and Chapter 2 is to sell you on the idea that you can redefine success for yourself. We no longer have to conform to an old-fashioned model of success that has led us to hustle for our value and prove that we are good enough. The old model is not working for women.

> "You never change things by fighting the existing reality. To change something, build a new model that makes the existing model obsolete." -R. Buckminster Fuller

That old definition of success, void of fulfillment, is unsustainable for most women. By redefining success we create a new model that is first and foremost rooted in fulfillment.

The most hopeful part about redefining success for you is that your success will be your responsibility and no one else's. It means that you do not have to conform to someone else's definition of success. You can create your own.

This also means that you get to decide whether you will take action or sit on the sideline of the arena of your life.

Success will look different for each woman, but it will feel the same—fulfilling.

Why Do We Need to Redefine Success for Women?

Why do we need to redefine success for women?

So that every woman can have a shot at success. It can't be an exclusive club for .000001% of women. We need equal opportunities for success.

I was speaking with Mary and I told her that I was writing a book that offers every woman an equal opportunity to feel successful.

She asked, "What's the title?"
I eagerly responded, *Redefine Success for Women, A Proven Blueprint to Design a Fulfilling Life*.

Her response was, "Well, I don't put myself in the category of success, so I won't even take a look at it." It hit me hard.

I wanted to rethink the title because most women have already made a decision about whether to choose success or forgo it. We don't vocally announce our decision, but we live by it. It becomes a core belief through which our other decisions are influenced.

We exclude ourselves from events or situations if we think they are meant for successful people. We think we don't belong there.

Or, on the opposite side, we walk in with a badge of honor because we've made a million dollars, all the while feeling insecure because our marriage is falling apart and it is hard being around other women who have thriving marriages.

It is an unannounced decision, a clouded narrative, of how we have inherited definitions of success based on our exclusive experience of it.

This is precisely the problem. We have labeled ourselves "successful" or "unsuccessful" based on the Poisonous P's success metric that has been ingrained in us since birth.

The Poisonous P's metric of success has become our truth, meaning, it is a deeply rooted belief that we have come to accept as our reality.

I was a stay-at-home mom with four kids under the age of four. I had learned to intentionally design every part of my life: my marriage, my home, my family, my friendships, and my health. I was intentional about trading success for fulfillment because of my pain, seeing my mother's "successful" life. To be unsuccessful became the compass of my decision. I was very intentional about creating a life that fulfilled me, which was the opposite of a "successful" life. And I felt fulfilled, at least for a while.

I didn't feel successful because I didn't have a social media following, a mansion, a fancy car, or a PhD behind my name. But I worked so hard to design a life that felt whole. I got up at 4:30 in the morning most days to prepare myself for my day. I was fierce about disciplining my mind and body. I said "no" to many good things, I was firm with my boundaries, and honored my need for a routine.

If you had asked me, "Do you feel successful, January?"
I would have answered, "No, but I am a good mom."

This means that my core belief was that I couldn't be successful if I was "just" a stay-at-home mom. Why?

An even deeper core belief that I held was that good moms lay their life down for success. Mothers had to put their dreams aside as a badge of honor.

Then there was Lisa. Lisa worked hard as a school teacher. Her students loved her. She gave her job 100%. Then she went home and took care of her kids, washed a mountain of laundry, helped with homework, made healthy meals, volunteered at her local church, drove everyone to soccer, made time to call a friend, and took care of her man. She worked so hard day in and day out to serve everyone. But if you asked her, "Do you feel successful, Lisa?" She would answer, "No, I am just a teacher."

In other words, the prevailing thought is that teachers, even though they give so much to their students, don't deserve to be successful. The Poisonous P's metric of success, once again, does not place value on our hard and sincere work to contribute to the lives around us.

This belief is poisoning our society.

Suzanne just got promoted to VP. She works sixty hours a week and comes home to take care of her kids and attends all their basketball games. She makes time to visit her aging parents and do her mother-in-law's taxes because she can no longer do it for herself. She runs a foundation to help kids who have been abused. She works hard on her marriage, even though she is not appreciated by her husband. She is giving so much, pushing herself to a point of burnout, but doesn't ever feel like it's enough. If you ask her if she feels successful, she would say, "I'm stressed and burnt out."

Suzanne might look successful from the outside, but she feels rotten on the inside. She feels like an imposter.

She has achieved a certain prestige and power before the world but lost parts of herself in the process.

When people praise her success, Suzanne offers only a guarded smile, because she doesn't want anyone to know that she is a fraud.

Life is not what she was promised. Her success doesn't feel good.

Our current model for what makes a woman successful isolates hard-working women who give their blood, sweat, and tears to serve everyone else around them.

It is unfair for Mary who would not have picked up this book because she automatically assumed that she was not part of the .000001 % of the exclusive elite "successful" club.

It is unjust that Lisa, who is giving 100% as a teacher, doesn't see herself as a successful woman.

It is sad that Suzanne, who is burning the candle at both ends, can't celebrate all that she has accomplished because she is burnt out and unappreciated.

I believe our current definition of a successful woman contributes to women's self-doubt. We can't just allow good-hearted souls who give so much of themselves to doubt their goodness or doubt if they are even good enough for a successful life.

They doubt their goodness, they doubt their contribution, and they doubt their worth.

At the very least, they undermine the belief that what they offer the world is even valuable.

By redefining success, we give every woman an opportunity to pursue the things that make her feel happy, and not just conform to irrational cultural demands of what success "ought" to look like.

Redefining success is about honoring each woman and her unique and irreplaceable value in the world.

Every woman should have a deep, subconscious belief that who she is and what she offers the world, no one else can.

Every woman is unrepeatable.

You deserve a life free of doubting your value.

So, how should we redefine success?

The Purpose of a Successful Life

What is your purpose for achieving your goals?
Why do you want to be fulfilled?
What would bring more meaning into your life right now?

The simple answer is, to give of yourself.

Let me build my case.

Tony Robbins said it best, "The secret to living is giving."

Why? Because giving brings meaning to your life. When we bring value to someone else's life, it makes us feel significant. It gives us evidence that we are needed by someone.

Simon Sinek offered a simple but real example of this in a motivational video, explaining why "acts of generosity" are good and important. In this speech, he explained that after helping a stranger pick up his dropped papers in the streets of New York City, he felt "good." The man he had helped was surprised and grateful. Then another random stranger, who had witnessed the kindness, also thanked him for his act of generosity. Sinek pointed out that there is a "feel-good" hormone called oxytocin, which is released when we do something kind or generous, and it makes us feel good. And as Sinek said, "Oxytocin binds humans."

Our ability to contribute to the lives around us fulfills our human need for meaning.

> "It is not what we get but who we become, what we contribute...that gives meaning to our lives."
> –Tony Robbins

Success that is sustainable must be integrated with our purpose, which is to contribute who we are to the world.

Our new model for success cannot be divorced from our purpose. In other words, I cannot feel successful apart from who I was fashioned to be.

The old model of success is all about "me," my world, my life, my needs...me, me, and me.

An old movie quote from Bette Midler sums it up best, "But enough about me, let's talk about you...what do YOU think of me?"

The irony is that what makes us happy is to live selflessly.

The purpose of our 'purpose' is to give of ourselves, that is what makes us happier human beings.

Regardless of what you choose to do in this world, your purpose is rooted in contribution.

Giving is what brings the simple joy that we all crave.

Therefore, success cannot be selfish. Rather, what makes success so rewarding is when we can say, "I am not the end, but rather a means to a greater end, which is to contribute to the lives around me."

The purpose of becoming a successful woman is to maximize your contribution to humanity.

The more we give, the more we receive in life, and the more we feel fulfilled. The more meaning we have in our lives, the greater capacity we have to bring meaning into other people's lives.

Therefore, a successful woman who understands her purpose to contribute is burdened with the responsibility to give back to the world.

The purpose of success is generosity.
Generosity brings meaning into our lives.
Generosity makes us feel alive.

We want so much to give of ourselves because it is entwined with our purpose as human beings.

BUT....how can you give without first receiving?

Most women don't have a "giving" problem, but many of us do suffer from a "receiving" problem. Meaning, you can't give from an empty cup. Unless you are intentional about receiving the nourishment that you need for sustainable generosity, you risk burnout.

We live in a burnout culture, not because women are not giving, but because they are unaware of their need to receive.

Unless we receive, we cannot sustainably give, which means we are incapable of filling another's cup.

We expect women to give and give without empowering them to create a lifestyle of receptivity, and that is a big problem.

The new model of success has to integrate purpose, generosity, and receptivity.

So, on to the next question: What is receptivity?

Receptivity is our willingness to receive guidance and growth that nourishes us from within. It has to be from within.

Receptivity means:

"I am coachable."
"I receive feedback and harvest from it."
"I seek role models intentionally."
"I am reading and expanding my mindset."
"I am learning from my mistakes."
"I am building new skills."
"I am intentional about resting and taking care of myself."
"I am processing my experiences and growing from them."
"I am a student of my own life."
"I am praying, meditating, and listening to myself."

In other words, I am investing in myself and in my need to continually grow.

If what makes us fulfilled is giving, then we have to be intentional about receiving.

Success, therefore, requires us to both give and receive.

Guideposts to Redefining Success

I have proposed a new definition of a "successful" woman.

The new definition of success is rooted in fulfillment first, while in pursuit of our achievements, in harmony with our unique purpose.

This new definition gives every woman an equal opportunity to live a successful life.

It is no longer an exclusive club for the .000001% of women, but rather, for all women.

We all deserve a shot at success.

This new definition includes YOU in whatever season of life you are in. It includes your daughter, your mother, grandmother, sister, friend, co-worker, boss, and all the women in your community who have doubted their unique purpose.

This new definition of success is inclusive, and it is up to you.

If you want it, you can have it, regardless of the profession you choose.

This new definition of success will be your new standard of how you are going to redesign your life moving forward.

Success is achieving fulfillment while growing in harmony with your irreplaceable purpose in every season of your life.

I want to invite you on a journey to personally define what success means for you—it has to be personal.

I am going to give you some guideposts to consider and process. Take your time to wrestle with old beliefs, identify the beliefs that no longer serve you, and deepen your awareness of new beliefs that will help you create a fulfilling life; a life fully alive.

Find the courage to let go of old beliefs that are holding you back from the life you want.

Take a stand for your life, it is the only one you've got.

5 Guideposts to Redefining Your Success:

- Guidepost #1: Success Cannot Be Divorced From Your Purpose
- Guidepost #2: Success Requires a Dream
- Guidepost #3: Success Requires You to Personally Develop Yourself
- Guidepost #4: Success Requires a Life of Wholeness
- Guidepost #5: Success Requires a Mentor

Guidepost #1: Success Cannot Be Divorced From Your Purpose

What good is achieving so much if it does not align us with our purpose in this world?

Your purpose is the very reason why you are here on earth. It is your unique contribution to the world. It is what gives your life meaning because you are fulfilling your call. Your success can not be void of your purpose.

You and I know of women who have achieved so much, and yet feel empty inside. We feel empty when we are not in harmony with our call. The irony is that we go through decades of education without being trained to consider our unique purpose in every season of life.

"Purpose" has become a grand, big, untouchable thing in the sky that everyone seems to know we need to pursue, but no one seems to be teaching us how to pursue it.

Your purpose doesn't come to you from external forces, it has to be discovered from within. Your purpose is revealed by digging into the deepest, most sacred desires of your heart. Yet, unless you know how to ask the right questions and are trained to develop yourself, you could spend your life hoarding achievements that are void of the very reason you are alive.

No wonder so many women are void of life. It is because they are void of purpose. Your purpose gives you life.

Your purpose is the DNA of your contribution, it reveals what fulfills you.
To deny your purpose is to deny who you are.

What would happen if Mother Teresa, who had such a passion to serve the poor, had ignored her purpose? I wonder how many more people would die unloved, unknown, and unseen? The fulfillment of the deepest desires of her heart became a window to her call to build the Missionaries of Charity.

In living out her purpose, she inspired the world.

My purpose at this moment as I write this book is to build a training school so women can be whole, while simultaneously cultivating an intimate relationship with my husband Ryan, and prioritizing the formation of our children to become wholesome adults. It is also my purpose to create a peaceful home, deepen my friendships, honor my rest, become a student of myself, and develop my ability to lead. My purpose is not solely on the macro, but also the micro-moments of my day-to-day life. My purpose is to achieve what I feel called to do at this moment, in tandem with my purpose to be the mother and wife I was created to be.

My purpose is to make my ordinary moments extraordinary.

If we are to redefine success for women, we have to break the old model that "purpose" is a grand word that has nothing to do with our present moment. Our purpose has everything to do with the present moment. It is living with a vision that is in harmony with who we are created to be, while also being intentional about our contribution in the present moment.

By thinking solely of achievement, we could miss the tender opportunities that fulfill our hearts and make us feel alive.

Our purpose in the little moments of life is equally as fulfilling as those grand moments...perhaps even more.

Guidepost #2: Success Requires a Dream

Every Friday, my children know that it is movie night because mommy and daddy keep date night sacred.

Date nights quickly became dream nights. During this time together, we would dream about the life we wanted and design every part of our life—together. This is the glue that keeps our marriage sweet even after sixteen years, eight children, and building a business.

One date night, we sat at our local Irish pub and started dreaming. We were tired of the busy life in the DC area and dreamt of a simpler life, ideally by the water. We took one step and explored what we didn't think was possible, because of Ryan's geographically based real estate business. The idea of moving six children into an unknown state where we knew no one and had no source of income felt like a massive risk. It was borderline crazy.

That dream took us on a quest. We traveled up and down the coast of Florida where we found the most perfect place to raise a family. At that moment, my heart was sold on a new dream: the dream to simplify our life, start a business together, and be close to the water.

We decided to move in two years. The two years of preparing, praying, and planning our move to Florida was one of the most challenging seasons of our marriage, and yet, it was the most rewarding.

Dreaming comes before discipline.

REDEFINE SUCCESS FOR WOMEN

Our dream to move to Florida took us out of our comfortable life in Virginia so we could pursue the dream of the season.

There were real moments of struggle as we fought to pursue the dream we both shared. And yet, the vision gave us life.

We had a clear vision and we lived in such hope, knowing we were making our dream a reality.

This is a picture of me writing a future post on Facebook and writing about our dreams accomplished. It was bold.

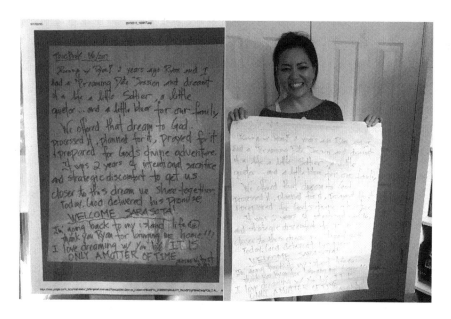

We never looked back.

Dreaming comes before discipline. Pursuing a dream that felt impossible inspired me to grow into someone I had never been before.

I had to train my mind, my body, and my spirit in order to fight for our dream to move to Florida.

I had to deepen my skills of saying "no," managing critics, protecting my dream, planning, focusing, and a whole lot more.

When you are inspired by your dream, you will lay down your life for it, dying to your old self and giving birth to a new woman.

Your dreams are simply the bait to becoming your greater self.

Without a dream, your heart becomes stagnant and weary.

So, what is a dream?

A dream is a radical vision of something you deeply desire to pursue that you have not achieved before. It reveals a deep desire in your heart and it calls you to become greater than your current self.

A dream is a radical vision that comes from the deepest desires of your heart.

Your desire is your North Star.

Your dream reveals your destination. It is the compass that leads you to your greater contribution, therefore it is what fulfills you.

Without a dream, you remain the same woman year after year, unable to reach new heights of possibilities. To not dream is to risk not fulfilling your highest purpose.

Success, rooted in fulfillment, requires you to have a dream of the season.

Every season of life requires you to live a vision because without a vision you will perish into a slow death of quiet desperation.

If you are single, there is a dream waiting to be uncovered.
If you are a new mom, you have a dream within you.
If you have reached the pinnacle for your company, there is a dream ready to take you to the next level.
If you are an empty nester or retired, there is a dream waiting to be discovered.

Every season has a unique and irreplaceable dream because every season of life has a unique purpose that only you can fulfill. The dream for each season is the path to fulfilling that unique purpose in that season of your life.

When the dream is clear, you simplify your life and focus on what matters most.

Guidepost #3: Success Requires You to Personally Develop Yourself

To me, the most dangerous words in English are, "I know." Because "I know," translates to, "I don't need to know more." In other words, you do not need to personally develop yourself. You have already arrived at your highest and best self. Yet, we know from a very logical level that there is always room to grow.

Personal development is all about growth. Growth, in simple terms, means receptivity. It means that you are personally developing your mindset and skill set to progress into a higher version of yourself. Success cannot be stagnant, it must be rooted in growth if the goal is fulfillment.

To be fulfilled, you have to invest in your personal growth.

Tony Robbins puts it simply, "If you are not growing, you are dying."

Success becomes dangerous if we feel like we have arrived, and there is nothing more we can do to grow. Success ought to be a constant evolution to our higher self.

I was speaking to a 67-year-old lady and asked her, "How are you growing as a woman? What skills are you developing in your life now?"

Her response was, "I don't need to grow. I raised good kids, I don't need to know more. I think at this point, January, I've learned everything I need to know to be a woman."

I learned so much from that exchange.

She was a very powerful example of who I don't want to be, and I was grateful for this encounter, which led me to make a decision about how I want to grow old: I never want to be too prideful to grow. I want to be old and still willing to learn more. I want to learn from all types of people—from children, from my students, and those who seemingly can teach nothing.

When we observe, study, and harvest insight from the lives around us, we don't just grow in knowledge, we grow in wisdom. When we grow in wisdom, we gain a greater capacity for contribution, which ultimately fulfills our need to give more of ourselves.

We grow so we can give.
When we give, we feel fulfilled.

> "Only by giving are you able to receive more than you already have." -Jim Rohn

It's ironic, isn't it? That it is in receiving that we are capable of giving?

The secret to giving more of ourselves is to personally develop who we are.

When we are skilled in conversation, making people feel important, drawing firm boundaries, planning, or managing our minds, then we can give more of ourselves.

Personally developing our mindset and skill set is a prerequisite to our contribution, which leads to greater fulfillment.

How can we maximize our capacity to personally develop ourselves?

Humility!

- Humility is the secret ingredient to personal development.
- Humility comes from the root word humus, a rich dark soil in which things can grow. Humility is taking responsibility for our need to personally develop our mindset and acquire new skills.
- Humility is the secret ingredient to receptivity.
- Humility is not about being small, it is about taking responsibility and ownership of your growth.
- Humility is about receiving, it is about being a student of life.
- Humility is about learning from other people.
- Humility is about receiving constructive feedback.
- Humility is growing from your critics.
- Humility is being patient with your progress.
- Humility is knowing you don't know enough and you need to continue to learn.
- Humility is having mercy and kindness for your mistakes.
- Humility is harvesting wisdom from your failure.
- Humility is knowing you have not arrived, and that you are constantly evolving.

- Humility is celebrating other women around you and not being jealous of their success.
- Humility is looking at your life and regardless of the poor decisions you have made in the past, you choose hope and make it better.
- Humility is learning a new skill when you feel like you've mastered so many.
- Humility is being gentle with yourself.
- Humility is knowing when to take a step back or when to lead the way.
- Humility is knowing when to push yourself and not give yourself excuses.

Humility is attractive. It is inspiring and it makes a woman beautiful. A woman who is humble enough to grow can achieve self-confidence that can light up the room.

A humble woman is a powerful woman because her power is from within.

Miss Angie was in her late 60s when I was coaching her. I was in awe of her humility.

She lived a beautiful life and served her children with the utmost love and respect. She helped build her husband's business and was a wellspring of wisdom to so many souls around her. Yet, when I was on a coaching call with her, she took notes as though she was a novice, hungry to learn and grow.

What humility!

I want to be like her when I grow up. I want to have enough humility to continually receive wisdom and nourishment from the people around me.

I want to die as a student of life.

Her example has become the new standard by which I want to hold myself accountable. I want to spend the last years of my life learning and sincerely harvesting wisdom because there is always so much more to know.

Socrates remains relevant yesterday and today.

"The more I know, the more I know that I don't know." -Socrates

Imagine going to an architect. After he hands you a carefully mapped-out floor plan, do you expect your house to be ready in a week? It sounds laughable, but that is sometimes what we expect in our own journey. The construction and development of a fulfilling life will take time, with failures in between.

Failure will be your source of wisdom.

Part of our family creed that we say every day is, "I fail forward fast and learn from it." Failure is your compass to greater wisdom.

When we are intentional about designing every part of our life, we will quickly realize how much personal development and growth are required for us to achieve the design and the dream that we want.

Guidepost #4: Success Requires a Life of Wholeness

Where do you learn how to design a life of wholeness? Wholeness is sort of a buzzword; we kind of know what it is, but we have not defined it for ourselves.

What is wholeness? Wholeness is being fully alive in every part of our life while growing in harmony with our original design; our purpose.

And wholeness has everything to do with intentionally designing every part of your life.

In college, I was a lost soul who had suffered the pain of being disgusted with herself. Those were the only words that I could use to describe how I felt: I was disgusted with myself.

I was steeped in comparison. I was insecure. I was anxious, stressed, and I wanted to run away from my life. It was my belief then that I could not change anything about myself.

It was my first month in college that I met Elena. In my first meeting with her, she asked me, "What kind of a woman do you want to be?" I laughed and said, "Do I really have a choice?" Her matter-of-fact response was, "Yes, let's design you."

I can still hear my own nervous laughter. The idea of "designing myself" might as well have been Aramaic, because it was the first time I had ever heard of it.

But, because I was so broken, I accepted her mentorship and did everything she told me to do, and more. The excruciating pain I felt in my life made me hungry for mentorship.

For three and half years, I met with her almost every month. She helped me design me, by giving me concrete and practical homework. I wrote these designs on a small piece of paper and carried them with me. We called it, "My blueprint to wholeness."

My first lessons were:

- Homework #1: "Make my bed before I go to the bathroom." With this, I began to develop discipline.
- Homework #2: "Wake up at 4:30 am to pray, plan, and meditate." This allowed me to prepare my mind.

- Homework #3: "Get rid of comparison and competition," so I could be free to engage in meaningful friendships. This quickly healed my loneliness.

Next, I had to write a routine that honored sleep, nutrition, my need for exercise, prayer, quality friends, and my environment, as well as my mental and emotional health. Elena wanted to make sure that I was intentional about filling my cup in every arena of my life.

Elena held me accountable. Every month, I showed her my progress.
She trained me to see with eyes of wholeness.
She helped me design myself.
She taught me to be intentional about everything.

Apart from Elena's influence, I'd had no training regarding routines, boundaries, dreams, planning, or decision-making.

This is why I teach what I teach: I am the fruit of what is possible when we begin to see life with eyes of wholeness. Elena gave me this gift, and I have used it to train thousands of women. I teach them how to design a life of wholeness, a life fully integrated and alive.

And it makes me wonder: why do not teach our children to design a life of wholeness so they can get a head start in their own life?

Imagine building your dream house without a floor plan. You just build it as you go, hoping it will miraculously be the house that you want for yourself. It would be insane to build your dream house and pay hundreds of thousands of dollars to build it, without first consulting an architect to help you create the floorplan for the house you want.

And yet, we build our life without consulting a mentor, and without a clear vision of the life we want.

- We cross our fingers and hope for the next available job, not the job we really really want.
- We hope to marry Mr. Right, without knowing what we want and don't want in a man.
- We hope to create an inspiring, perfect family, without knowing how to manage our minds, our time, our routines, and our homes.
- We hope to find friendships that nourish us, without clarity of our standards of the kinds of friends we want to surround ourselves with.

Why does the idea of having a blueprint for life seem so foreign to so many of us? It seems like common sense but is far from common practice.

Some women even rebuke the idea of designing every part of our life. So first, I want to identify why we resist designing a life of wholeness.

The biggest reason is that we don't know how.

We have been programmed to disintegrate and compartmentalize parts of who we are. Seeing with eyes of wholeness shatters those old beliefs, and that makes us feel uncomfortable.

Figure 3.1

WHOLENESS ARENA

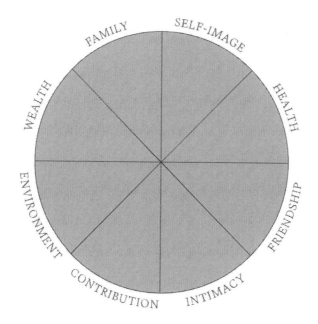

Go to redefinesuccessforwomen.com for a free printable download.

We are either living by design or by default. Ultimately, it is our choice.

The reason why so many of us feel like parts of us are being broken is that we have failed as a culture to train women to see with eyes of wholeness and design every part of our life with greater intention.

Look again at the Arena. Which part of your life feels hard and challenging right now?

Ask yourself:

- Who was my mentor in this arena?
- Who taught me the skills I needed to make that part of my arena fulfilling?
- Who held me accountable for growing my mindset in that particular arena?

The response is usually...that no one showed you how.

It is not your fault that parts of your life feel empty, when no one ever showed you how to fill them. We need to stop blaming ourselves for the choices we were never taught to make.

My bold dream is to offer mindset and skill set training to help our young women design a life that is whole.

Success rooted in fulfillment cannot be void of a life by design, a life that is whole.

In the next few chapters, I will guide you in the process of designing each part of your arena, so you can achieve wholeness.

Guidepost #5: Success Requires a Mentor

Do you know that you make 35,000 decisions a day?
Yet, there is no mentorship on how you can develop your decision-making skill.

We make the most important decisions of our life without proper mentorships. Decisions such as the kind of friends I surround myself with, finding work that I love, communicating in relationships, managing a home, and getting along with people at work.

These are not insignificant decisions, these decisions alter the quality of our life and yet, most of us make these decisions alone.

It used to be that humans lived near family. Grandmothers, aunts, and uncles could give sound and wise advice on decisions and major life choices. But now, we no longer have that infrastructure to support us in a life of wholeness.

Why are women abandoned to a life without proper preparation and then judged based on their "perfection"?

Do you expect Simone Biles to win a gold medal on her own without a coach? No.

Then why do we expect women to live life well, without proper mentorship?

The fastest way for you to achieve what you want is to ask someone for help.

If no one is mentoring us to design a life of wholeness, is it our fault that our careers are pushing us to burnout? Or that our marriages are ending in divorce? Or that our kids are falling into the trap of drugs and alcohol?

No. At least not completely.

Are we expected to be infused with a special grace of knowledge to know how to communicate effectively as a wife after we walk down the aisle?

Do we receive a magic wand of knowing how to take care of our children the moment they are delivered? No.

We are designed to have mentorship in our life.
Without it, we risk squandering the short time we have.

I am the fruit of mentorship. Without it, I would have spiraled into my own brokenness. I cannot even imagine where I would be without Elena.

Her mentorship changed not only my earthly life, but I'm convinced, also my eternal life. I don't even want to imagine where I would be without her guidance.

Her mentorship became the fuel that led me to create the Wholeness Coaching School, where we train others and give them everything they need to build a business as a mentor.

I was convinced that if we created a business where women could mentor other women, we would rebuild the culture. So, that is what I did.

I created our signature Masterclass, which trains women to design a life of wholeness. We trained mentors, most of whom came to us without previous coaching or business experience. Students gathered in small groups and were trained together.

Our Wholeness Coaching School grew 1000% in our second year. To me, this was evidence of the hunger for mentorship. Women want fulfillment, and our program proved to be a worthy investment toward their fulfillment.

This model has transformed communities, families, schools, and relationships. Thousands of testimonies across forty countries prove that there is a hunger for mentorship, and the testimonies are nothing short of miraculous.

The next section provides a window into the formulas we use in our school...

The Fulfillment Formula

Figure 3.2

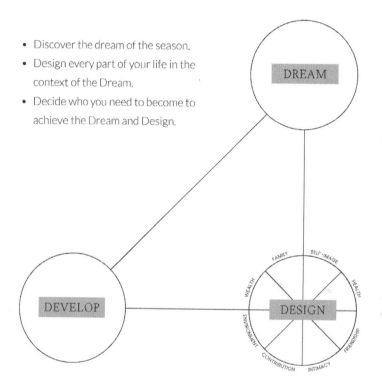

FULFILLMENT FORMULA
Formula to Becoming Fully Alive

- Discover the dream of the season.
- Design every part of your life in the context of the Dream.
- Decide who you need to become to achieve the Dream and Design.

Go to redefinesuccessforwomen.com for a free printable download.

I want to introduce you to the Fulfillment Formula.

This formula is something that you can use over and over again, in every season of your life. You can use this blueprint as a single woman, married, mother, empty nester, retiree, CEO, or teacher—this is available to every woman.

This is a blueprint for a fulfilling and meaningful life; a successful life.

This formula has been used by thousands of students across the world, helping them to design a life of fulfillment.
If you use it, you will never look back.

The Fulfillment Formula is your blueprint for cultivating a fulfilling life.

It is composed of three parts. I call it the trifecta.

1. Dream—A radical vision of something you want to accomplish.
2. Design—Intentionally creating a life of wholeness.
3. Develop—To achieve your dream and design, you need to continually develop yourself to become the woman you want to be.

Every part is equally important.
Each part hinges on the other.

You can't have a dream without creating a life of wholeness. That design is the infrastructure you need to pursue what you are called to pursue in your particular season of life, without compromising parts of who you are.

At the same time, you can't design a life of wholeness without the vision of the dream you are striving towards.

The dream and the wholeness design hinge on your ability to personally develop yourself. Who do you need to become in order to achieve the dream and design for your life? Your ability to grow your mindset and skill set will determine your capacity to achieve the life you want.

In 2019, I had a dream to make a million dollars in the first year of my business, as a mother of six. So, I intentionally designed a life of wholeness that would hold me accountable. I knew I had to prioritize parts of my life as I went on my quest to pursue my dreams.

This is how I designed every part of my life as I pursued my dreams.

My Wholeness Design:
- Self Image: A loving mother, disciplined with my routine.
- Mental and Emotional Health: Resilient against critics.
- Physical Health: Cut sugar intake and walk 3x a week.
- Spiritual Health: Daily prayer and greater intimacy with God.
- Friendship: Connect with friends who are business owners and mothers.
- Intimacy: Weekly date nights and go away every quarter.
- Contribution: Learn how to create online courses, and study marketing daily.
- Environment: A peaceful home and remodel my children's rooms.
- Wealth: Make a million dollars in a year. Expand the business.
- Family: Be present to my children, and make family time sacred.

I knew that if I achieved my dream to make one million dollars in a year, yet I became stressed, overwhelmed, and was not present to my children, or neglected my home, my friends, or my husband, I would not have tasted the fulfillment that could come from making a million dollars over that first year.

I made my first million after eighteen months! I celebrated for a hot minute, but what fulfilled me most was that the journey itself had been so rewarding and fulfilling.

I am not trying to impress you but to impress upon you that big dreams are possible with discipline, a clear design, and a concrete plan. It takes hard work and determination to make the journey just as fulfilling as the destination.

Achieving our dreams while prioritizing our life of wholeness is what our hearts truly long for because the journey is what fulfills us. The destination is glorious but the journey ought to be sweet.

A life of wholeness requires discipline, simplicity, and focus.

Achieving our dreams is in harmony with our purpose.
It is rewarding.

Achieving them in the context of a life of wholeness is the fulfillment that allows us to taste the joy, peace, and freedom in knowing that life is meant to be beautiful.

You are worthy of a fulfilling life.

You were created to have more life in your life.

Be determined.
Be vigilant.
Be intentional about doing the interior work, and you can have it all.

This formula will be your secret weapon for life!

In the second half of this book, I am going to walk you step by step through the Fulfillment Formula: how to dream, how to design a life of wholeness, and how to develop who you need to become to be fully alive.

The New Model of Success is Rooted in Fulfillment

Success now has a new metric that is rooted in fulfillment.

We can begin to invite women to shift the conversation of success from achievement to fulfillment.

We can invite women to begin their fulfillment journey so they can become who they were created to be.

No more comparison.
No more competition.

We can celebrate each other as we begin to unearth our unique call in the world.

When someone asks you, "Do you feel successful?" Instead of imagining your bank account, or your social media following, you get to imagine every part of your life working in harmony with your dream and your life of wholeness. You get to imagine a woman who is personally developing herself to grow to new heights, achieving things she never imagined possible.

Here is the new metric:

I feel fulfilled when…

- "I am clear and growing toward my unique purpose in this season of my life."
- "I have a clear vision of the dream I am intentionally pursuing."
- "I am intentionally cultivating a life of wholeness to support my dreams."

- "I am personally developing myself, growing both my mindset and skill set to achieve both the dreams and wholeness design for my life."
- "I have a mentor who is holding me accountable to fulfilling who I am created to be in this particular season of my life."

Fulfillment is not perfection, it is a journey of progress.
Be patient with your growth.

If you have never lived your life with such a clear intention, then there will be a time of transition where you will need to first build the foundation.

It takes time to grow.
Rome was not built in a day.

But that is a great temptation, especially for those who struggle with perfection. You will struggle and wrestle with your old self in order to give birth to your new self. Your new self is a woman who is taking responsibility for the life she wants. Your new self is a woman who is fierce about life by design.

Growth sometimes means death to your old self, but growth means there is life after death.

You are not stuck as long as you are willing to *train-up* for it.

You deserve to feel successful.
Every woman deserves to feel successful.

Success is first and foremost rooted in fulfillment. This is our new metric of success!

Unfulfilled People Become Toxic to Our Community

Caution.

Unfulfilled people can become toxic to our communities.

I was dropping my son off at work and a man who I thought was an acquaintance started asking me about my upcoming speech with Ed Mylett and John Maxwell. I told him how honored I was to be on the same stage with my mentors, who are some of the most influential people of our time.

He went from 0-10 and burst out in anger. "John Maxwell is a fraud! Ed Mylett is ripping people off! You are toxic to women!"

He was screaming at me in front of my three-year-old son. I was shocked.

The fierce January, who is typically not shy about voicing her opinion, crumbled in tears. I could not believe that this man, who I thought was a friend, could ever treat someone this way.

Later, his wife apologized. She told me about some internal struggles he was having: struggles with his family, his career, and parts of his life where he was hurting.

Hurt people hurt other people.

When parts of our lives are unfulfilled—maybe because we refuse to grow and heal—we risk projecting our pain onto those around us.

When parts of our lives are unfulfilled, we are susceptible to comparison, judgment, rage, sadness, shaming, and criticizing other people.

We can become jealous monsters capable of lies and deceit.

This man took his frustrations about the different parts of his arena out on me.

I became a victim of his unfulfilled life.

I learned a lot from this toxic experience; I learned that each of us has a duty to fill our cup, otherwise we risk becoming toxic to the people around us, especially those who are close to us. An unfulfilled life is like a volcano waiting to explode and cause havoc.

What's more—it is only a matter of time until unfulfilled people become toxic to themselves.

Therefore, we must live lives of wholeness that bring fulfillment to our souls. By investing in our own personal fulfillment, we can invest in filling other people's cups, instead of robbing them of it.

So, where do we begin?

How to Begin to Design a Fulfilling Life

Where do you begin to design a fulfilling life?

1. Begin by deciding to invest in your life of wholeness. This decision is essentially an investment in the people you love. You cannot give what you do not have, so your growth will determine the quality of your relationships.
2. Find a mentor to hold you accountable for designing a life that is whole. Olympians don't just happen, they are surrounded by coaches who help them achieve their goals. You are in the Olympics of your life! And your gold medal is fulfilling who you were created to be.

It is far too great of a risk to do things on your own, without accountability. Ryan and I have allocated part of our income for mentorship because what would take us three years without a mentor, will take us six months with one.

Find a mentor who understands the integration of every part of your life. Find a mentor who believes in a life of fulfillment. Commit to investing in mentorship for the rest of your life and then give back, and mentor those around you.
Find a community to support you. We need women around us who can encourage us to dream, design a life of wholeness, and personally develop ourselves.

We are social human beings. We thrive in a community. What better community to be part of than women who are dreaming and growing together? If you want to join our Woman School community, go to thewomanschool.com and join our masterclass. Sign up for a dream session with one of our certified strategists, who will walk you through how to begin designing your life.

What I offer here is just the beginning. I cannot possibly give you everything you need in just one book. If you want to go deeper, I invite you to train with us in designing a life that is whole.

Over the next few chapters, I will walk you through the Fulfillment Formula. I will walk you through specific exercises to help you discover your dream, design a life that is whole, and learn how to personally develop yourself.

You have to work at it. Life by design requires time, effort, energy, and massive action. Most of us have been conditioned to live by default. I can help you lay out a beautiful blueprint for your life, but unless you work on yourself, nothing will change.

> "If you want to have more, you have to become more. For things to change, you have to change. For things to get better, you have to become better. If you improve, everything will improve for you. If you grow, your money will grow; your relationships, your health, your business, and every external effect will mirror that growth in equal correlation." –Jim Rohn

It is very important to remember that building takes time. Once you have outlined your design, that is when the real work actually begins.

P_{AUSE}

P_{ONDER}

A_{CT}

Chapter 3

1. How would success that is rooted in fulfillment influence the way you make decisions in the future?
2. What do you believe is the purpose of a successful life?
3. How does an unfulfilled woman become toxic to her community?

CHAPTER 4

SUCCESS REQUIRES A DREAM

---

1. I Don't Know How to Dream
2. Dreams vs. Goals
3. Why is it Important to Fulfill Your Dream?
4. What is the Dream of the Season?
5. Three Reasons Why Women Are Not Dreaming
6. What if I Have Never Had a Dream?
7. How to Discover Your Dream Now

I Don't Know How to Dream

Here are a few thought-provoking questions about dreaming. As you answer, rate yourself 0 - 10; 10 being a resounding "Yes," 0 being a brutal "No."

1. Can I identify my dream right now in less than three sentences?
2. Do I know the difference between dreaming and goal setting?
3. Is my current circle of friends intentionally pursuing their dreams?
4. Who is holding me accountable for pursuing my dreams?
5. Do I know how to dream as a skill?

I suspect that these questions are not easy to answer.

Most of us have seen the hashtags and the social media posts that say, "Chase your Dreams!" Some of us look at an encouraging quote like this and for a hot moment, feel empowered. We respond with a battle cry of, "YES! I am going for it!"

Yet others will glance at that quote and shrug it off because it is irrelevant. They've reached a point in their lives where "dreaming" feels childish, immature, irresponsible, and not really practical. They've concluded that some are dreamers and others are doers, as though they exist in opposing realities. Ultimately, they've given up on the idea that we are to live our life with a vision.

Part of the problem is that there is confusion about dreaming. Women are told to pursue their dreams but have not ever been shown how to dream. There is a cataclysmic difference.

Empowering a woman to dream is very different from equipping her with the skills to dream.

Dreaming is a skill.

The bigger problem is that we are not training women to build skills. Skill is the ability to do something well, be it typing, driving, cooking, budgeting, holding boundaries, and yes, dreaming.

Skills expand our choices in life and yet, there is a massive void in skill training in our education system, and even in our homes.

We need skills to enter the workforce.
Mothers need skills to manage their homes.
Friends need skills to avoid toxic relationships.
Intimacy requires skills to cultivate a healthy relationship.

Whatever job you have will require you to *skill-up*. And the more skills you can compound together, the more choices it will give you in your life.

If you learn the skills of speaking, writing, marketing, and managing people, more doors will open for you.

The more skilled you are in decision-making, planning, holding boundaries, effective communication, and managing your mental, emotional, and physical health, the greater chance you have to achieve your dreams.

Skills give you choices.

On the contrary, a lack of skills will make your dream hard to attain. So, where did you go to learn the skill of dreaming?

When I train a woman on how to discover her dream of the season, it is usually a challenging journey at first. It is challenging because she first needs to build her dreaming skills before she can discover her dream. Dreaming requires imagination, patience, and focus. And if these muscles have been dormant, then we first need to awaken them.

If you have not learned how to dream before, then dreaming could be met with resistance. However, once the muscle of dreaming develops, a world of possibilities opens.

So stay the course.

The rule is that dreaming comes before discipline. When a woman understands the power that dreaming has to develop discipline in her life, she won't look back.

My goal is to help you discover your dream of the season. I want to bring a deeper awareness to the mindset you need to unearth your dream right now.

First, what is a dream?

To help me explain what a dream is, I will clarify the distinction between dreaming and goal setting.

Dreams vs. Goals

Figure 4.1

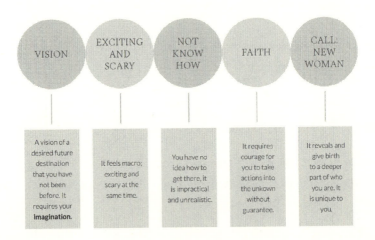

Go to redefinesuccessforwomen.com for a free printable download.

I am going to use the chart above to help explain the difference between dreams and goals.

What is a dream?
A dream is a radical vision of something you deeply desire to pursue that you have not achieved before.

It reveals a deep desire in your heart and it requires you to become greater than your current self.

A dream can only be discovered by maturing the deepest desires of your heart. In order for your dream to be fulfilling, it needs to be in harmony with your highest good, your purpose.

The purpose of your dream is to discover your unique purpose in your specific season in life. The dream is designed to reveal your call. Who you are called to be must be in harmony with your Universal Desire for the good, not apart from it.

If your dream is to rob a bank, that is not life-giving. If your dream is to be a pop star because you want everyone to adore you, that is not life-giving.

But if your dream is to become a pop star so you can contribute good to the world, then that is a noble dream, in harmony with a universal desire to contribute good to the world.

Motivation does matter.
If we are to design a successful life that is rooted in fulfillment, we have to be certain that our motives align with our higher purpose.

You can't bring darkness and expect to live a fulfilling life.
It is counterintuitive.

You are made to bring light to this world and doing so will make you feel alive. The fact that giving makes you feel good is evidence that you are made for contribution.

For your dream to be fulfilling, it has to be rooted in contribution because that will bring you the joy that you ultimately desire.

Your dreams are not born mature, they need to be developed.

I used to dream of a nice car. But as I realized the purpose of my life, the car was no longer as significant to me as dreaming of a school for women. As I grew in maturity, I realized that building a school that transformed women was far more rewarding than a nice car.

I can still like the nice car, but I am no longer attached to it, it has lesser significance. The point I am trying to make is that our dreams need to be nurtured and matured, to grow in harmony with our universal desire to bring good.

These are the five elements of a dream:

Element #1: A Vision

A vision is a desire for a future that you can see with your mind and heart but that you have not yet achieved. Seeing it will require your imagination. Having a vision means that you are clear about where you want to go, and you can imagine yourself there before you even have a path to get there. It is the vision of a future that inspires you.

When I was 21, I had a vision of creating a school where women could learn skills that I was never taught in school. Skills such as saying "No," creating boundaries, living in gratitude, planning, and managing emotions. I imagined a school that would equip women with practical tools to help them design every part of their life. I was convinced that if there was such a training school, we would have less burnout, stress, and anxiety. I imagined a school for myself because growing up, no one taught me how to show up as the woman I wanted to become, and I suffered for it. I wished there was a place to learn how to be a woman...so I imagined one.

I drew a school for women on a piece of paper. It was a tall building with a gym on the bottom floor so students could exercise their bodies while they were developing their minds. I shared it with my friend Chelsea; to this day she still remembers the fireplace next to my desk where I drew my vision.

Fast forward two decades and here we are. The Woman School is now in forty countries with thousands of students across the globe. We equip women with mindset and skill set training to design a life that is whole.

Once upon a time, it was a dream.

It first lived in my imagination.
It felt impossible...ridiculous.
Yet I kept that vision in my heart, creating what was possible in my thoughts first.
I fought my own self-doubt to learn to walk in faith.

After sixteen years of marriage, and eight children, we are running a multi-million dollar company that has expanded to include The Man School, The Wholeness Coaching School, and The Woman School en Español.

The impossible dream was even bigger in reality.

> "Imagination is more important than knowledge, for knowledge is limited, whereas imagination embraces the entire world."
> —Albert Einstein

As children, we are encouraged to imagine. As we grow older, we are encouraged to put aside our imagination so we can become practical and start living as adults. We have implicitly created a narrative that maturity requires us to give up our imagination so we can finally grow up.

Amazon was once imagined in Jeff Bezos' vision. An electric car was once imagined by Elon Musk's vision. The Woman School was once just a dream—I felt I had no right to imagine this vision, but I did anyway. I had nothing to lose.

How many "impossible" dreams are we witnessing in our world today?

The things that have been created around us were first created in someone's imagination.

> "The imagination was given to us to create. That is where everything starts, it starts with our marvelous mind." —Bob Proctor

Imagination is a vital muscle that needs to be developed in order to pursue our dreams.

Without a vision, we perish.

A vision inspires us to push through challenging obstacles.

A vision is what gets us out of bed.

Our imagination allows us to dare to do the impossible.

Element #2: Exciting and Scary at the Same Time

The dream feels so impossible to you that it excites you and scares you at the same time. It is exciting because achieving it will dramatically impact every part of your life. But it is scary because it is so big that it makes you feel vulnerable.

It is exciting because it unearths the deepest desires of your heart, and by achieving it, you will never be the same again. You can feel it in your gut. But it is scary because it feels laughable and absurd. You can't seem to see how you could ever achieve it, but if you could, it would forever change you.

I train women how to dream. I use the word train very specifically because my students have to take action and condition themselves to get to a point where they can give themselves permission to dream of the impossible. When I walk a woman through discovering the deepest dreams of her heart, I can hear the excitement and fear in her voice. It is a mixture of feeling giddy while not being able to say it out loud because it feels so vulnerable. I can usually tell when we've hit the dream of the season because it awakens a part of the woman in a way that it brings out the child in her. It is like tapping into your childlike imagination skills and finally permitting yourself to be that little girl again.

It is such a privilege to witness a woman voicing her dream...it gives her newfound strength and courage.

But the path to discovering the dream can get rocky. It is all part of the process of unearthing something massive.

When I first allowed myself to dream of writing a book, my stomach would turn at the mere possibility. I had so much I wanted to share with the world, but because I struggled with English grammar as an immigrant, I told myself that I was a bad writer. I never imagined that I could write a book, much less a bestseller.

Yet, I decided to go for the impossible, and the impossible dream became a bestseller, This is Me, the Me I Choose to Be. The process was exciting and scary every step of the way. I realize now that the dream was mere bait to becoming a greater version of myself. To achieve something I had never achieved before, I had to grow into someone I had never been before.

I had to learn grammar...haha.

Element #3: Don't Know How

Thomas Edison once said, "I have not failed 10,000 times, I've successfully found 10,000 ways that will not work."

Edison didn't know how to build a lightbulb, but he persisted anyway. The "how" eventually showed up, but not before thousands of failures in the process.

When the Wright brothers decided to turn their bike mechanic skills into a flying gadget, they had to live in their imagination. No one saw what they saw in their minds, and people ridiculed them for trying—until one day, they succeeded.

Dreams don't come with directions or manuals. But it is precisely because you don't know how to achieve them that you have to develop a new mindset and skill set and become a new and elevated version of yourself in order to achieve it.

Not knowing how requires you to *train-up* and then the "how" will show up.

Not knowing how is the secret ingredient to becoming more resilient, resourceful, expansive, creative, and patient. For you to achieve your dreams, you first have to develop who you need to become.

Your dream becomes the bait to becoming your greater self.

Dreaming is such a force for greatness.

Element #4: Faith

Faith is moving forward into the unknown without guaranteed results. Pursuing our dream requires us to risk believing that it might come to fruition.

We don't dream because we do not want to be disappointed.
But the irony for women who are afraid of being disappointed is that they spend the remaining years of their life wondering what could have been possible had they dared to dream. It is a deep ache of regret.

> "The mass of men live lives of quiet desperation."
> –Henry David Thoreau

Faith is required to live a beautiful life, otherwise, we remain stuck in the comfort of doing only what we know is possible. It seems easy at first but the pain of regret creeps in. Faith means believing in the impossible regardless of the obstacles that may come our way.

Faith requires us to hope in things that we have not yet seen come to pass. And yet, to live without faith is to risk not living at all.

Element #5: The Call

Our call is a unique commission.

When we were born, we were created with a specific mission that only we can fulfill. Our mission is something we carry deep in our souls and we discover it through the deepest desires of our hearts.

Before I met Elena, I didn't know how to be a woman.
I didn't know how to say "No" to toxic relationships.
I didn't know how to honor myself.
I didn't know how to draw boundaries, which caused much suffering.
I didn't know how to manage other people's opinions of me.
I didn't know how to eat healthily.
I didn't know how to speak effectively.

The fulfillment of Elena's call became the seed for me to pursue my call to serve women. If she had not fulfilled her commission, I may never be writing this book and The Woman School would not exist.

The fulfillment of her call led me to fulfill my own call, and for that, I am eternally grateful.

We all have a unique and irreplaceable call, and it is through dreaming that we begin the journey of discovering our unique commission.

When we fail to dream, we risk missing the very purpose for which we were fashioned. The dreams that we hold dear in our hearts will reveal to us the very call that will fulfill us.

What is a Goal?

A goal is a specific intention to achieve something measurable and attainable. Goals allow us to set specific milestones on the way to achieving our dreams, and they help us to mature into the women we need to become to achieve our dreams.

Figure 4.2

ELEMENTS OF A GOAL

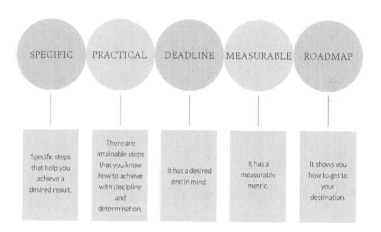

What is a Goal?

A Goal is a specific intention to achieve something that is measurable and attainable. Goals allow us to set specific milestones on the way to achieving our dreams and they help us to mature into the woman we will need to become. Our goals become our roadmap to the destination of our dream.

SPECIFIC	PRACTICAL	DEADLINE	MEASURABLE	ROADMAP
Specific steps that help you achieve a desired result.	There are attainable steps that you know how to achieve with discipline and determination.	It has a desired end in mind.	It has a measurable metric.	It shows you how to get to your destination.

Go to redefinesuccessforwomen.com for a free printable download.

Our goals are the roadmap to our dreams.

Goals are part of the dream, but they do not inspire us like the dream does. Goals are necessary because they are the micro-steps to help us achieve our dreams, but we should not confuse our dreams with our goals. Otherwise, we could spend our life only goal setting, but not fulfilling our dreams.

I often hear the terms "dreams" and "goals" used interchangeably. I think this confusion leads a lot of women to set a goal but not truly understand the importance of pursuing a dream that feels impossible. As a consequence, women don't feel inspired, even if they reach their goals. Goals do not necessarily require us to become an elevated version of ourselves—they require discipline but not so much our imagination, vision, or faith.

Goal setting is a very important skill to achieve our dreams.
But it is important to create a clear distinction between goal setting and dreaming.

Elements of a Goal:

- Element #1: Specific—Each goal is specific and clear.
- Element #2: Practical—The goal is attainable and there are clear steps to achieving it. This requires discipline.
- Element #3: Deadline—There is a specific date to accomplish the goal.
- Element #4: Measurable—You have a metric that holds you accountable.
- Element #5: Roadmap—You have a step-by-step plan to get to your desired outcome.

At first, it could take a while to understand the distinction between "dreams" and "goals," but once you understand the distinction, it will change the way you look at your life moving forward.

When I train a woman to dream, and I ask her what her dreams are, it is usually the case that she is simply goal-setting. I can hear in her voice an ache of unfulfilled desires that she has no language for.

When women understand the distinction between dreams and goals, then they can see the connection between their sense of restlessness and their lack of a dream.

When our dreams are unclear, we feel a sense of angst in our hearts. We have no words for it.

We say things like, "I feel like something is missing, but I can't put my finger on it. I feel like I'm stuck."

But even these words are often left unspoken.

Dreaming is a vital skill to learn if you are to live a fulfilling life. We can't feel alive unless we are growing toward who we were created to be. Living the deepest desires of our hearts—having a dream—is not foolish or childish. It is the most mature thing we can do to fulfill our call.

Perhaps, we ought to be like children again, and learn to dream.

Your Dreams and Goals Now

Here is a sample of dreams and goals. In our school, we give women formulas they can replicate and can use over and over again to discover the dream of the season.

Figure 4.3

Go to redefinesuccessforwomen.com for a free printable download.

Take some time to ponder your own dream and the goals that would be required to achieve it. Write them down. Be specific.

If you want guidance, go to thewholenesscoachingschool.com to find trained and certified woman school strategists who can help you.

Why is it Important to Fulfill Your Dream?

The most important reason why a dream fulfills us is because somewhere in that dream is the seed of your unique and irreplaceable contribution in that specific season of life.

Let me explain.

When we first started The Woman School, it was a massive leap of faith. It was a dream. My husband sold his company so he could jump in as CEO and I could train and build courses. We had six children and no income, just our savings that we invested to start a business from scratch.

We had to make some difficult choices that impacted our comfortable life. I had to let go of help, which was so crucial at the time with six little ones. We had to be careful with money, so the usual things that we were accustomed to doing as a family—such as eating out and taking adventures—had to be put on hold. For a year and a half, we barely made any money while building the business.

My son was not happy. He was upset that we left our comfortable lifestyle to pursue our dreams. He saw the long hours we put in, even after everyone else was in bed. He witnessed the early mornings. But he also saw that we prioritized the family and our marriage. He saw the joy we had in our hearts even though there were some real struggles that we had to endure. He would tell us, "You should not have given up your old business to start a new one."

Ryan would respond, "I gave up my work life to pursue my life's work, and I love it. Don't worry son, this is what it means to dream."

The first year was brutal. But after eighteen months we made our first million dollars, and our son Jack was able to witness the journey.

I told him, "This is what it means to pursue a dream that leads you to fulfill your life's call! You, too, will have to sacrifice if you want to achieve your dream to play professional golf."

Our children may or may not follow what we tell them, but they do study how we live our lives. Our lives become the blueprint by which they make decisions on how they will live their life.

The way you live your dreams will become the foundation of how they live theirs, for better or for worse.

The dreams that we hold dear in our hearts reveal the purpose of why we are here. If we do not risk discovering and carrying out that dream, we risk losing parts of ourselves.

I got to model for Jack why mothers need a dream.

I can't look at him and say, "Son, go chase your dream and follow the call in your heart," if I gave up on mine.

Mother or not, working or not, we each have a duty to fulfill our dreams if we are going to live a fulfilling life.

Our life's call makes us feel alive because when we are growing in harmony with who we were created to be, we are in alignment. Regardless of the struggles that come from growth, we feel joy.

This is a joy that comes from the hope that we are moving toward who we were created to be.

One of my favorite quotes is from St. Catherine of Siena, "Become who you were created to be, and you will set the world on fire."

Your dreams can set your heart on fire.

Your dream could become your greatest contribution to the world. To not dream is to miss your opportunity to be the light you were created to be.

To live a life of contribution is to live a fulfilling life, a life that allows you to wake up every day with deep gratitude, knowing you are creating an impact in the world.

A dream is the vision of a life we dare to pursue. Without a dream, we start to doubt if our life even matters.

You are an unrepeatable woman and what you offer is irreplaceable. Your contribution becomes part of the tapestry of life. Your role is massively important. Without your contribution, there is a void no one else can fill.

Regardless of what you choose to do in your life, if you want to be fulfilled, then you must dare to discover the dream of the season.

What is the Dream of the Season?

We don't have to live in the past or wait for the future. We can't wait for retirement or for our children to grow up to pursue our dreams.

If you don't have a dream in every season of your life, then it is easy to feel a sense of restlessness that you are missing something.

We can't blame women for feeling uninspired or living only for vacation or the weekend. Unless someone is teaching women how to dream, chances are, life has become mundane. Day-to-day life becomes drudgery. There is very little to look forward to, which makes scrolling through social media an easy temptation.

Sadly, that just exacerbates the problem.

If I had decided to forgo my dream because I had five young children at that time, I would have missed my opportunity to reach women in forty countries right now. Each dream in each season of life has led me to the next dream.

It is only when we take the first step that the next step is revealed.

If, right now, you do not know what your dream is, then perhaps you are missing your contribution in this season of your life.
Maybe you are feeling restless and anxious, but you don't know why.

Because no one is training us how to dream, it is not our fault.
We don't know what we don't know.

It is very important to note that we cannot judge other women's dreams.

Someone's dream could feel like a goal to you but might be massively huge to her. We are not judges. We are the cheerleaders and accountability partners of our friends.

We can shift the conversation from "chase your dreams" to "pursue your dream of the season." This shift can give a woman in any season of life a reason to pursue her life's unique call at that specific moment.

We don't need excuses. We need mentors to help us give birth to our dreams. We need women who are fulfilled because they are pursuing their dreams.

Three Reasons Why Women Are Not Dreaming

#1 No Training

Most women don't know how to dream, because they've had no training.

Dreaming is a skill, but it is hard to find training that specifically walks women to discover the dream of the season.

#2 Stress

Stress makes us selfish. Selfish because it is hard to focus on other people's needs when we are just trying to survive.

Stress feels like you are being chased by a lion. When you are being chased by a lion, that is not the time to ponder your dreams or think strategically about how to design a fulfilling life. All you are doing at that moment is trying to stay alive.

Stress puts us in "survival mode." It hijacks the imagination and inhibits us from pondering our unique contribution.

How do you manage stress?

You have to learn the skill of managing your mind. You cannot control the external circumstances in your life, so the only path to a stress-free life is to learn how to manage your thoughts.

#3 Comparison and Competition

Women fail to dream because they have developed a bad habit of comparing themselves to other women. This makes them feel inferior. Comparison is toxic because it builds walls between your relationships, causing you to feel lonely and devalued.

Comparison is similar to any bad habit—it is ingrained and you automatically do it.

At some point in our youth, when we started to feel insecure, we compared ourselves to others and developed a habit of looking at other women to either make us feel good or bad about who we were.

Comparison cripples us to such a point that we believe our dreams could never be possible.

Comparison leads to loneliness and unfulfillment.

How do we break this bad habit? Awareness, training, and scripts.

What if I Have Never Had a Dream?

Then you have to be patient with yourself.
And be gentle.

You are building a new muscle.
Begin with knowing what you want and don't want to put up with in your life.

Allow yourself to observe the desires of your heart.

Find a mentor who will hold you accountable while pursuing your dreams. Also, find a community that will walk with you on this journey.
You are not alone.

It is never too late. You are just a few skills away from imagining what is possible.

Begin with what you want.

How to Discover Your Dream Now

Are you ready to dream?

I will walk you through exercises that thousands of women like you are using to discover their dream of the season.

Something to note as we go through these exercises:

1. YOU MUST BE VULNERABLE: If you have not given yourself permission to dream, this might feel uncomfortable—that is normal. You have to push through it if you want a shot at discovering your dreams.
2. THIS IS A JOURNEY: Discovering your dream of the season is a journey of awareness. For some, they will know what it is right away, but for most women, it is a long journey of self-discovery.
3. THE DREAM NEEDS TO BE NURTURED: You wouldn't hand your newborn baby to strangers. When you discover your dream, protect and nurture it, and share it only with the right people. Otherwise, you risk being convinced to not go for it. Surround yourself with people who feed your dream, not rob you of it.
4. THE DREAM REQUIRES MASSIVE ACTION: Identifying the dream is only half the adventure. You then have to take massive action to give birth to the dream.
5. THE DREAM WILL TAKE TIME: When you are dealing with unknown circumstances, you don't have a guaranteed outcome. But remember, that is part of growing in faith. Time will reveal so much for you.

The D5 Life By Design Formula

The "D5 Life By Design Formula" is what our Woman School Certified Strategists (coaches) use to walk their clients through deep discovery. It is a powerful formula that guides our students through the very practical process of designing their life.

These are the five steps in the Design Formula. We offer deep training in each area.

1. D1—Desire
2. D2—Dreams

3. D3—Design
4. D4—Discipline
5. D5—Detach

Figure 4.4

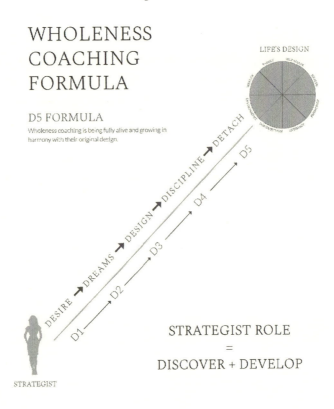

Go to redefinesuccessforwomen.com for a free printable download.

I cannot share the depths of this process in this book because that would be a book in itself. What I want to do here is to show you replicable formulas that you can use in every season of your life.

Exercise #1. Dream Expansion

Below is the "Dream Expansion" worksheet. Follow along and jot down your notes. There are no right or wrong answers, just be honest!

On this worksheet, you will note three types of dreams:

Figure 4.5

DREAM EXPANSION

Use the table below to fill out your possible, stretch, and impossible dreams. Once you have written the dreams that come to your heart, circle or highlight the impossible dream that stands out the most to you.

POSSIBLE DREAM	STRETCH DREAM	IMPOSSIBLE DREAM
A dream you have achieved before or for which you have a clear idea of the steps.	A dream that you have not achieved before and would be challenging, but you understand the steps required to achieve it.	A dream that feels scary and exciting. You do not know how to get here, but you really want to achieve it.

Go to redefinesuccessforwomen.com for a free printable download.

1. The Possible Dream—A dream you have achieved before, or for which you have a clear idea of the steps.
2. The Stretch Dream—A dream that you have not achieved before. This dream would be challenging, but you understand the steps required to achieve it.

3. The Impossible Dream—A dream that feels scary and exciting. You do not know how to get there, but you really want to achieve it.

Use the above worksheet to fill out your possible, stretch, and impossible dreams. Spend some time with your answers. Is there a dream that stands out? Which one? Make the decision; pick one dream. Then use the worksheet below to process the dream you chose.

Exercise #2: Imagining Your Dream

Below is the "Imagining Your Dream" worksheet.

Figure 4.6

IMAGINING YOUR DREAM

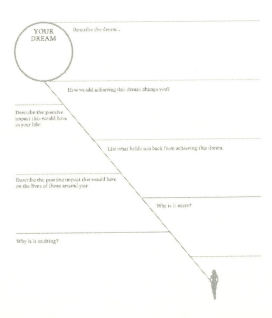

Go to redefinesuccessforwomen.com for a free printable download.

The directions here are simple:

1. Once you have identified and decided on your dream, write it again here. Describe it vividly, with as much detail as you can.
2. Answer the following questions:
    - How would achieving this dream change you?
    - List what holds you back from achieving this dream.
    - Why is it scary?
    - Why is it exciting?
    - Describe the positive impact this would have on your life.
    - Describe the positive impact this would have on the lives of those around you.

How do you feel after imagining your dream?

Exercise #3: 145 DGA, Planning for the Dream
Below is the "145 DGA: Planning for the Dream" worksheet. This is probably the most used worksheet we have across all our schools.

The "145 DGA" stands for one Dream, four Goals, and five Action steps. This is a one-page blueprint to help you create a plan and move it into action. This will simplify how you achieve your dream.

Figure 4.7

145 DGA
1 DREAM, 4 GOALS, 5 ACTIONS

DREAM
Write a concise statement that clarifies your dream.

GOALS
Identify key goals that will help you achieve your DREAM. In the second box, write the deadline for each goal.

ACTIONS
List the ACTIONS necessary to achieve each GOAL.

Go to redefinesuccessforwomen.com for a free printable download.

It is time to plan for the dream!

When you first work on your action plan, you may feel absurd, as I did. But, the process of writing it out, and wiring the possibility in your mind, will eventually take you from absurd to possible. This process is part of taking something massive and infusing it into your Reticular Activator System—repeatedly—until you start to see the possibilities.

When you fill this out, it is not the time to edit or censor your dream. It is a time to live in your imagination. Most women stop the dream long before they allow themselves to expand what is possible. But right now, you are just living in your imagination, so don't limit yourself. Simply observe how this dream makes you feel.

"145 DGA" Instructions:
1. Write your dream at the top. This should be a concise statement that helps clarify the dream.
2. Identify four key goals that will best help you to achieve your dream. Underneath, write a deadline for each goal.
3. In the five boxes under each goal, list the actions that will help you achieve each goal.

This one-page plan, your 145DGA, is your blueprint. You can use this over and over again. It combines your dream, goals, and action plan on one page for you to review every day.

Get a Woman School Strategist (coach) or find an accountability partner to hold you accountable and you will see a whole new world unravel before you.

Next, it is time to design a life of wholeness.

Let's begin.

P_{AUSE}
P_{ONDER}
A_{CT}

Chapter 4

1. What dream have you been holding back that scares and excites you at the same time?
2. Why do you think it is important to fulfill your dream of the season?
3. How does creating a distinction between dreams and goals influence the way you plan for your future?

CHAPTER 5

SUCCESS REQUIRES A LIFE BY DESIGN

1. Old Belief = "You Can't Have What You Want"
2. Why Skill is the Bridge to Having It All
3. What Does "Having It All" Mean To You?
4. Ground Rules For Designing a Life of Wholeness
5. Designing a Life that is Whole
6. Fulfillment is Your Choice

Figure 5.1

FULFILLMENT FORMULA
Formula to Becoming Fully Alive

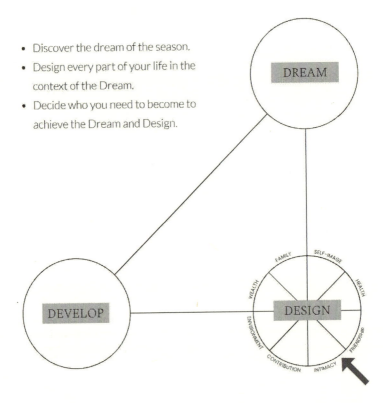

- Discover the dream of the season.
- Design every part of your life in the context of the Dream.
- Decide who you need to become to achieve the Dream and Design.

Old Belief = "You Can't Have What You Want"

The idea that you can design and redesign your life the way you want it sounds intriguing, but you probably doubt that it's realistic.

A common narrative is...

"It is childish and unrealistic to assume that I can have everything I want."
"I don't have a choice—I just deal with it."

"Some people are lucky—I'm not."
"I've done everything I could, there is nothing else I can do."
"I can't change myself, I was born this way."

Over the next few pages, I want to challenge these beliefs and convince you that you can have the life that you want.

I understand if you are doubtful, but give me a chance to prove to you that you have a choice. I will walk you through this new belief.

Figure 5.2

Reticular Activating System

Remember the *Reticular Activating System (RAS)*? It is working hard for you. It is looking for evidence of exactly what you tell it to look for.

If you say, "I can have it all!" or "I can't!" that is what your *RAS* will help you find.

If you repeatedly focus on what you don't want, you will continue to live the life you don't want. Think of the people in your life who complain about everything no matter the circumstance. They seem to not like their life year after year.

These people have neurologically built a habit of focusing on what they don't want, so that is exactly what they see more of.

The awareness of your *RAS* is a game changer.

You can replace old beliefs in the same way that you can learn a new language, by putting some effort into replacing your limiting beliefs through the process of neuroplasticity.

Neuroplasticity is the brain's ability to change and adapt due to experience.

Our brains are made of billions of neurons that fire and wire together based on our experiences. When you were born, you did not know what a cup was, but through the process of repetition, you understood what a cup was. This process happens through neuroplasticity.

> **"Neurons that fire together, wire together."**
> **–Donald Hebb**

Think about how you learned how to type. You had to consciously remember where the letters were and through the process of repetition, you could eventually type without looking at the letters on the keyboard. Your brain created neural connections and through the process of repetition, hardwired them subconsciously.

If I ask you where the letter "b" is on the keyboard, you might not know where it is, but if you put your finger on the keyboard, your finger will probably find it faster than your brain can. You had to put the effort into consciously wiring the keyboard placements to make those neural connections.

Through the process of repetition, you create neural connections and in time they subconsciously get hardwired in your brain.

This process is the same process that you go through to reprogram limiting beliefs that no longer serve you.

No matter what wiring you have now, no matter what narrative you tell yourself, you can rewire new beliefs and reprogram your mind with new ideas that can serve you better.

> "Whether you think you can, or you think you can't, you're right." –Henry Ford

Whatever script you have programmed for yourself, you will find it.

When you have a limiting belief that you cannot design every part of your life with great intention, then you will find a million reasons why you can't.

But if you believe that you can redesign your life, then you will find all the many ways you have never seen before because now, your RAS is helping your brain find what you want.

You can use your RAS to reprogram old beliefs and create new beliefs that can help you design a fulfilling life.

If you want to believe that you can have the life you want, then the first step is to begin by imagining, "I can have the life I want."

You have the choice to shift your limiting beliefs:

FROM: "It is unrealistic to assume that I can have everything you want."
TO: "Who are the people that are living life by design? What can I harvest from them?"

FROM: "I don't have a choice, just deal with it."
TO: "I have a choice to find new strategies to achieve the life I want."

FROM: "Some people are just lucky—I'm not."

> TO: "Luck is What Happens When Preparation Meets Opportunity." –Seneca (Philosopher)

FROM: "I've done everything I could, nothing will change."
TO: "What skill do I need to grow to help me overcome this challenge?"

FROM: "I can't change myself, I was born this way."
TO: "I can rewire negative beliefs through neuroplasticity."

Neuroplasticity is your new friend.

Why Skill is the Bridge to Having It All

First off, have I shifted your belief that it is possible for you to have it all?

Have I at least convinced you that if you replace old limiting beliefs then maybe, just maybe, you can have the life you really, really, really want?

Before you answer that question, I want to share with you *The Tale of Two Mountain Climbers*.

Two mountain climbers were each presented with a ten million dollar reward that was waiting for them on top of a mountain. All they needed to do was climb to the top and the reward was there for the taking.

It was neither a race nor a competition between the two climbers. Each woman had her own ten million dollars on top of the mountain.

Mountain Climber #1 was an unskilled climber. She looked at the mountain and was petrified, but the idea of a ten-million-dollar reward was enough bait to make her accept the offer.

But, she had no idea where to begin. She never learned how to use a rope, harness, or helmet. She had no training in how to study the terrain. She was not physically prepared so her endurance was low, to begin with. She didn't even have the right shoes. But, the ten million dollars was enough to get her to try anyway.

She grumbled her way through the climb, finding all the reasons why this was an impossible task. She made it 1/10 of the way but she was too beat up and exhausted to keep going. The whole experience was overwhelming. She repeatedly spoke self-defeating scripts, such as, "There is no way I can do this. I am so horrible at this. I am going to fall. This was a ridiculous idea—I can't even believe I fell for it. The ten million dollar reward must have been a scam! No one can climb this."

Eventually, Mountain Climber #1 gave up her ten million dollar reward.

Why? Because she did not have the right mindset or skill set that she needed to make that climb. No one showed her how, and she never made it a priority to take the time to learn. Instead, she gave up the ten million dollars that would have changed many circumstances in her life.

But it didn't stop there. She was angry and quickly blamed everyone else for encouraging her to believe that this was a possible track for her. She convinced those close to her to not believe the "lie" that there might actually be ten million dollars waiting on that mountaintop. She was bitter.

Her ten million dollars is now wasted—no one else can have her reward.

Woman Mountain Climber #2: Skilled Climber

Mountain Climber #2 looked at the mountain and she knew it is going to be a heck of a climb but she trained for it. She prepared her mind. She studied terrains, physically conditioned herself, and knew when to rest to refuel. She had the right gear and she had practiced getting up from a fall. She knew it was going to be a challenge but she pushed herself in ways she never imagined she was capable of.

Because she was prepared, she knew that she would eventually get to the top, no matter how hard it was. She had trained her mind to focus on what she wanted and had acquired the necessary skill to get her to the top of the mountain. She wrestled with her own fears but scripted her way out of them.

She never gave up. She was bruised and bloodied, but she kept going until she reached her reward! The ten million dollars was hers!

As she soaked in her surroundings, she saw that the view from the top of the mountain was beyond her wildest dreams—the view alone was worth the pain and sacrifice.

When she was asked, "How does it feel to get ten million dollars?"

Her response went like this, "It is great. But to be honest, I am proud of myself because I never imagined I could scale such an impossible mountain. It feels so good to achieve something I never realized was possible. Plus, the view from the top is surreal—I want everyone to scale their own mountain. It is so worth it. I want to encourage every woman to *Train-up* so she can see this amazing view from the top."

Woman Mountain climber #2 got her reward, and in the process became a woman she never imagined was possible.

What is the difference between Climber #1 and Climber #2?

SKILL!

The difference is that one was skilled and the other was underskilled.

Skill is the bridge to getting what we want.

Skill is the difference between someone who gives up and someone who keeps trying.

We all have a ten-million-dollar mountain that is ours for the taking.

What is your "ten million dollar mountain" waiting for you right now?

Skill is the bridge between the life you have now and the life you want in the future.

Your skill is what allows you to scale new mountains in your life.

If you rewire your limiting beliefs and build new skills, then you can have it all—I call this "whole."

You can design a whole version of yourself.

What if this feels overwhelming?

If you feel like the life you want to design for yourself is overwhelming, then ask yourself, "What skill do I need to train myself to climb the mountain of my dreams?"

Life becomes overwhelming when we are underskilled.

Remember, overwhelmed = underskilled.

Let's talk about your skill training.
Where and how did you learn these skills growing up?

- Decision-making
- Communicating expectations
- Creating a standard for friendships
- Recalibration
- Saying "no"
- Communicating boundaries (7% Words, 38% Tonality, and 55% Body Language)
- Managing your mind
- Dreaming
- Routine
- Planning

Were you ever trained in these skills?
My guess would be no.

Why aren't we trained in these skills? Why is this such a massive oversight in our education system? No wonder life is so hard for so many women.

- It feels overwhelming to be in a new job if you lack the skills to communicate your needs effectively.
- It feels overwhelming for a new mom to have to learn thirty new skills while dealing with postpartum hormones.

- It feels overwhelming to expect a woman to make the most important decisions of her life without decision-making or boundary skills.

We are trying to heal broken marriages without accountability skills.

We are trying to solve the chaos in our homes without learning boundary skills, mind management, or time management.

It is overwhelming for any woman to solve the compounding problems in her life without skill training.

Life is just overwhelming when we are underskilled.

Any mountain (or even a hill), is daunting if you lack the skills to climb.

Is it any wonder that many of us feel stuck at the bottom of our mountain?

We are spinning our wheels, trying to solve our problems with a very limited skill set. Too often, our attempts look like the experience of Mountain Climber #1.

> "Insanity is doing the same thing over and over and expecting different results."
> –Albert Einstein

Every new season equals new training. We can't solve new problems with our old mindset and skill set. *That* is lunacy.

It is easy to doubt what is possible when we lack the skills to bridge the gap.

This is why we have a love/hate relationship with perfection.
We love the idea of it, which is why we are fascinated by images of perfection on social media.
But we hate it because we think it's a scam.
If we can't see ourselves doing it, then it must not be possible—it must be a scam.

We are secretly repelled by this so-called life of perfection—not because we don't want it—but because we feel like we can't have it. We turn to judgment and criticism instead of acknowledging that if we Train-up for it, maybe we could have that so-called "perfect" life.

It is irrelevant if it's fake or not. You have no way of knowing, and you can't jump to conclusions. What if it is real? What if it is possible? Does calling it "fake" make you feel better about yourself?

My point is, instead of being critical, we should find active solutions to model the good that we see in other women's lives. Just take the good.

It is easy to be judgmental and jump to conclusions when we have made up our minds that a beautiful and wholesome life is not possible for us.

Once, while I was on a date with Ryan, a man said to me, "You know January, I like seeing your perfect family, but it's fake. It's not real."

I used to get so brokenhearted when people judged me.

Perhaps this man did not realize how hard I train, both in business and for my family, to achieve the life I want. The reality is that I pay the price of discipline and work with intention to get what I want. I have cried tears of judgment, loneliness, and failure in order to rise back up again and redesign my life over and over again.

I do not give myself excuses to not discipline myself. Maybe people assume it's luck—but discipline does not feel like "luck" to me. It hurts.

We judge people based on what we think is possible. We mask our pain of jealousy by calling it fake. We limit not only what is possible for ourselves but also what is possible for other people, based on our own limiting beliefs.

But instead of judging, I propose we study what skills others have acquired, then emulate that in our own lives.

Skills make things easier.

When women come to me because they are overwhelmed, I ask, "What specific skill do you need to help you overcome this challenge?"

When we train ourselves to acquire new skills, we take what was once daunting and make it attainable.

It gives us a feeling of hope to know that we are not stuck—we are just a few skills away from attaining a life of wholeness.

However, it is important to realize that empowerment is not enough.

I believe in women's empowerment, but it is not enough.

Empowerment is just the beginning, it is not enough to help women create the life they want. We must equip them with skills.

Skills make the impossible possible.
Skills give you choices to design a life that is whole.
Skills are the bridge for you to have it all.

The shift of belief is...you can have it all as long as you are willing to *Train-Up* for it.

Training happens in the quiet, mundane, unglamorous moments.
Training requires us to deal with our wounds and do the necessary work to heal from them.
Training gives us permission to face our fears and failures.
Training musters the courage to forgive ourselves and those who hurt us.

Training is about consistency and taking action even when we do not feel like it.

Training is ultimately living a life of discipline.

We train daily because there is no end to self-mastery. This is a lifelong journey of *training-up*. It is NOT a "one and done" event. *Training is the secret ingredient to a beautiful life.*

Behind a beautiful life is a woman hard at work on her own discipline.

If you can shift your mindset, and accept the idea that you can achieve the life you want as long as you are willing to *train-up* for it, then you can have it all.

Your ten-million-dollar mountain is waiting for you.
If you are willing to *train-up* for it, it is yours for the taking.

It's that simple...though not easy.

This means the ball is in your court!

Discipline is your court, so *train-up!*

What Does "Having It All" Mean To You?

Let's define "having it all."

Consider again the architectural analogy of constructing your dream home: first, you need to create a blueprint of what you want, like a floor plan.

In the same way, you can't live the life you want *unless you first create a clear design* in your mind of how you want each part of your arena to look.

Once you have clearly articulated what a life of wholeness looks like for you, then you will have clarity regarding the skills you need.

In earlier chapters, I asked you to identify what you do not want to put up with anymore. That exercise was strategically designed to help you clarify what you wanted. By knowing what you don't want, it is easier to clarify what you do want.

Essentially, you are designing what a life of wholeness means for you. When you feel whole, it means that every part of your life has life.

This is what I call "having it all."

Having it All = Wholeness.

Definitions matter.

If we can define "all," as a life of wholeness, then having it all is not as complicated as we make it seem.

It is achieved by designing every part of your arena to match what you want, then developing the necessary skills to achieve that design.

We begin by carefully assessing each part of the arena and identifying how we can make it better. We then *Train-Up* with the necessary skills, scripts, strategies, and solutions to scale that mountain.

That's it?
Almost. ;-)

To be whole means that your cup is full in every part of your life.
It will look different for every woman but it feels the same—fulfilled.

Just to clarify...
Being whole is not pain-free. As a matter of fact, discipline is painful.
It also does not mean perfection.
It is having what we want while also enjoying it.

- It is not just about having your dream career, but feeling inspired in your career.
- It is not just about having a "perfect" body, it is about honoring your body regardless of what you look like.
- It is not just about looking confident, it is feeling competent.
- It is not just about having a fancy home, it is about having a place that inspires you and everyone who comes through.
- It is not about having hundreds of friends, it is about having friends who honor you.

Wholeness is not about perfection, it is about fulfillment.
It is loving who you are and what you have.

Wholeness, as we define it in The Woman School, is being fully alive in every part of your arena. It means that you are grateful for all that you have while also pursuing the life you want to have. It is not a contradiction, but rather an integration of being able to live in the present moment while also having a vision of a future you want. It is having both/and.

Because what good is achieving what we want and hating ourselves in the process?

Success is achieving the wholeness design that we want while also loving the journey of getting there.

"All" which translates to "whole," is something we universally desire. We all want to be whole. Wholeness is about your cup being full, full enough for you to pour into another person's cup.

A full cup = Full of Life = Fulfilled

You cannot keep giving from an empty cup. It is only when your cup is full that you can fill other people's cups without depleting yourself.

If you are not intentionally designing a life of wholeness then you are living by default. This means, whatever happens, happens.

If this is the case, you are not making life happen for you.
You are at risk of living your life based on other people's opinions of how your life should be.

It is easy to allow your mom, your dad, your cool friends, your boss, or even your husband to persuade you to live your life based on what they think is best for you.

And then you wonder why there is so much drama.

I used to be criticized by certain family members for the Montessori lifestyle that Ryan and I chose for our children. I tried to tiptoe around their opinions of how I should mother my children and it was mentally exhausting.

I had to *train-up* on new boundary skills so I could protect my peace from people who felt the need to share their opinions on how I raised my kids.

Don't get me wrong, feedback is important. But ultimately, we have to live our lives according to what we believe is best for us.

An example:
I choose a Montessori approach to parenting because it helped me teach my children internal autonomy with their decisions. I offered my children choices that would protect the joy, peace, and harmony that we wanted in our home. The Montessori lifestyle also informed the standard we wanted to create for our children.

We designed standards such as:

1. No negative labels, criticism, or making fun of siblings.
2. We contribute work in our home.
3. Dinner as a family is sacred, don't be late.
4. Degrading words are illegal.
5. Being a woman/man of your word is non-negotiable.
6. Your attitude opens or shuts doors for you.
7. Speaking with respect is non-negotiable.
8. Be mindful of your 7% words, 38% tonality, and 55% body language.
9. We are free to fail.
10. We make our beds every day.

Ryan and I train our children to neurologically wire new mindsets and skill sets by using scripts as a consequence. Some people might not agree with how we choose to parent our children and today, I know that is okay.

In the past, I felt so criticized for these choices. The criticism was hurtful but I learned to grow resilience.

Every family has their own way of doing things and we ought to respect our differences. I cannot allow other people's criticism to negatively influence how I design my family life.

The point I am trying to make is: unless you are clear on how you want to design your life, you are susceptible to other people's opinions of you.

When you are clear on what makes each part of your arena fulfilling, you can stand firm.

Ground Rules For Designing a Life of Wholeness

Before we get into the ground rules, I want to invite you to study the image of The Wholeness Arena. Each part of your arena is equally as important as the other; every part of you matters. When one part of your arena feels depleted, it will eventually bleed into the other parts because you are designed to be integrated.

By giving language to every part of your arena, you can give an accurate assessment and identify the part that needs your attention most. Use this image to help you determine how you are going to make decisions about your life moving forward.

Your task is to constantly pay attention to your needs, don't ignore them, but rather find solutions to help you overcome your challenges.

I am going to walk you through guideposts to help you design each part of your arena.

Remember, your design is unique to you alone—you have no need to compare yourself to others—but you can be inspired by how other women have chosen to live their life.

Figure 5.3

WHOLENESS ARENA

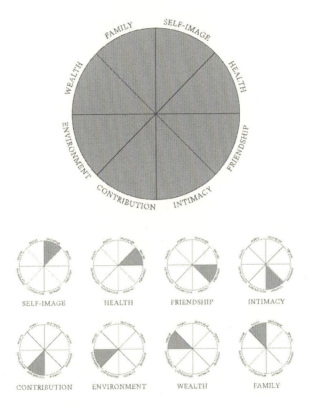

Before we begin designing every part of our arena, let's first establish some ground rules.

Ground rules to designing a life of wholeness:

1. TIME IS YOUR FRIEND: You need time. It is a journey of discovery and rediscovery and it takes time to unearth and wrestle with old beliefs that no longer serve you, so be patient. Patience is one of my struggles—I expect Rome to be built overnight! Even though I know change takes time, I still feel the burden of time because I can be impatient.

2. NOT AN ARRIVAL: You never arrive, you only evolve into a higher version of yourself. It is a constant evolution of designing and redesigning yourself with every season. What you want now could be different from what you want six months from now. As you grow, your desires grow with you. I can't pat myself on the back and say, "I have arrived! I've built a successful business as a mom of eight!"

   Why not? Because reaching one summit means that you are at the foothill of another mountain you have yet to climb. That is what makes this such a divine adventure.

3. *TRAIN-UP*: You can be whole as long as you have the humility to *Train-Up* and acquire the necessary skills to help you achieve the wholeness that you desire. You don't have to give yourself excuses.

4. YOUR WOUNDS BECOME YOUR COMPASS: We have all been hurt, but we can choose to be victims of our pain or find victory in our crosses. Your wounds can become a compass to your contribution in life. My own pain as a woman led me to this great work; my agony has become my greatest victory. It can be yours, too.

5. MENTOR-UP: If you desire a life of wholeness, you will need a mentor to help you get there faster. What you can do on your own in three years, you will do in six months with a mentor. It also guarantees that you will get to work. Mentors hold us accountable so we don't detour from our design.

Introducing the "Universal and Unique Design."

Figure 5.4

UNIVERSAL DESIRE AND UNIQUE DESIGN

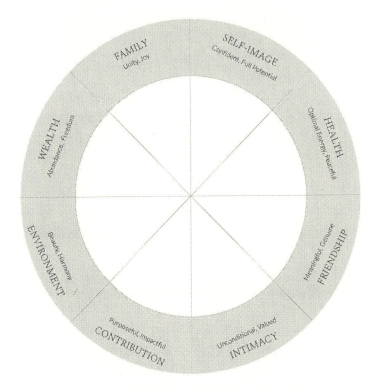

Go to redefinesuccessforwomen.com for a free printable download.

Let me explain this worksheet.

UNIVERSAL DESIRE: Universal desires are desires that are etched in our hearts and hold us accountable for growing in harmony with our purpose.

UNIQUE DESIGN: This is how *you* want to design every arena of your life. It is unique to you and your season in life.

The outer layer represents our universal desires as women (chapter two). Universal desires are desires that are etched in our hearts that hold us accountable to the fulfilling life that we all want.

The inner layer represents the life you want to design for yourself. It is unique to you and your current season in life.

The goal is fulfillment. In order to protect ourselves from unfulfillment, we want to align our unique design with the universal desire for fulfillment. You have the liberty to design every part of your arena however you choose to, but if you want to be fulfilled as a woman, then you have to align your unique design with the universal desire.

You can use the universal desires on the outer part of the circle to hold you accountable as you create the unique design within each part.

When you design each part of your life, ponder the universal design and ask yourself, "Is the life I am currently designing for myself in harmony with what fulfills me?"

The purpose of aligning your unique design with the universal desire is to ensure your fulfillment. Not everything that you want leads to your fulfillment, so this is why we check ourselves.

A quick example:
If you are tempted to design your health arena as, "I am able to eat whatever I want," but find that would be in conflict with the universal desire for optimal energy, then you need to tweak your design as a way to ensure your fulfillment.

Our universal desires hold us accountable to fulfilling the life that we really want.

It will take time to ponder and process, which is why you need a mentor to help you process each part of the arena.

In the next section, I am going to give you a brief description of each part of the arena as well as a guidepost to help you begin creating your unique design.

Remember to check your unique design with the universal desire so you give yourself the best chance at fulfillment.

When we redefine success to be rooted in fulfillment, we want to be intentional about every part of our life so that we achieve the dreams we are striving for while also living a life of wholeness.

Designing a Life that is Whole

Now we will go through each part of the arena to determine what you want so you can begin to create your unique design.

However, please note that what I am about to give you is only a cliff note version of The Woman School Masterclass where I train women on the mindsets and skill sets they need to design a life of Wholeness. But, this is enough to get you started.

If you are interested in learning more or having increased guidance and accountability, go to thewomanschool.com to learn about our signature Masterclass that took us to forty countries in under three years and landed us in Forbes Magazine. In the Masterclass, I walk you through an in-depth version of these guideposts.

Take this chapter of the book and retreat into a beautiful space where you can think and marinate on these concepts. They may seem simple at first but could feel like an impossible mountain to climb.

They may feel impossible because for some of us, this will be the first time we are hearing these ideas, and we have not yet developed the skills necessary to achieve them.

But, it is not impossible.
You can achieve a life of wholeness if you are willing to *Train-Up* for it.

Figure 5.5

WHOLENESS ARENA

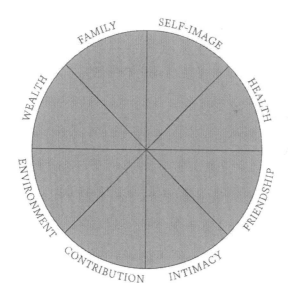

Go to redefinesuccessforwomen.com for a free printable download.

Let's begin with a personal assessment. Rate where you are in your journey to wholeness.

This wholeness quiz is a five-minute assessment of where you currently stand in every part of your arena. Go to thewomanschool.com to *"Rate Your Wholeness"* right now! (We recommend that you take this quiz, Rate Your Wholeness, every six months. As you are growing, so is your perception of how you view and see yourself and the world around you.)

At the end of the quiz, you will see a scale: Depleted, Stuck, Searching, Scaling, or Whole. These metrics are there to help you identify where you are now.

Remember, this is simply a starting point. The rest of your story is up to you...what will you do about it?

LET'S BEGIN DESIGNING EACH PART OF YOUR ARENA.

Remember: Your goal is to design a life of wholeness that fulfills you.

- STEP 1: I will explain each arena and give you a guidepost to help you think through your own unique design. I will also explain each universal desire so that you understand the importance of aligning your unique design with your universal desire.
- STEP 2: Create your unique design based on what you want in that part of your arena.
- STEP 3: Be certain your design is in harmony with the universal desire.
- STEP 4: Identify skills and strategies that would help you achieve your design.

- STEP 5: Consider how this will impact other parts of your arena.
- STEP 6: Write a list of possible role models.

Use the worksheets at the bottom of each section of the arena to help you outline your response.

SELF-IMAGE: The opinion that you hold of yourself.

Figure 5.6

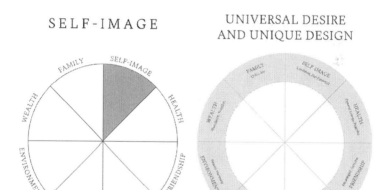

Do you ever find yourself using negative labels to describe yourself?
"I'm not confident."
"I am really bad with boundaries."
"I am so stupid."

What are the negative labels you use to personally describe yourself? Where did those negative labels come from?

- Maybe you inherited them from your mom's opinion of you growing up. Maybe she repeatedly called you "stupid," and as a little girl you didn't know how to respond, so you

neurologically inherited the negative label you are now carrying.
- Maybe you saw popular girls in school and labeled them confident, then by default, decided you were not confident.
- Maybe you had a bad experience with a boyfriend because you did not know how to draw boundaries. So instead of asking, "How can I hold my boundaries?" you applied that negative experience to all your relationships and labeled yourself as someone who is bad with boundaries. And because you labeled yourself as 'bad with boundaries,' you have used your Reticular Activating System to help you find the same kind of guy who takes advantage of you.

Do you see that the vicious cycle of a negative self-image can be inherited or acquired simply because you did not have the necessary training you needed to protect yourself from false labels that didn't serve you?

Your self-image is like a thermostat that you set for yourself. It doesn't matter how cold the outside temperature is, it recalibrates your temperature based on what you set it to.

What does this mean?
Whatever labels you have decided for yourself, you will revert to them because they have become your programming. These labels are the coordinates in the GPS, telling you where you are going.

But as you know, you can rewire a new self-image.

Align your Design with the Universal Desire: Confidence
We each have a universal desire to be accepted as we are. That is why we want confidence. A confident woman is free to show up as she is.

Confidence comes from competence.

A speaker becomes a confident speaker after she has worked on writing her speech, learning to connect with the audience, and mastering her intonations. These compounding skills lead her to be a competent speaker. Confidence, therefore, comes from competence.

We have a universal desire for confidence because we want to belong.

To be a confident woman, you just need to invest in your competence. Confidence that is built on a facade instead of skill training is not true confidence because true confidence can only come from competence. It has to come from within. You can be confident as long as you are willing to *train-up* for it.

Align your Design with the Universal Desire: Full Potential

We don't typically say things such as, "I want to live a mediocre life...." or, "I've chosen to waste my potential..."

What we do say are things like, "There is no point in finding my dream job because it's not practical..." or, "I am afraid to make the wrong decision, so I will wait until next year."

No one wants to waste their full potential.
But we are ill-equipped to maximize our potential.
We need skills such as taking massive action or recalibrating.

Sometimes we waste our full potential because we are afraid of being judged or because we are afraid of failing.

But, if you are willing to *Train-Up*, you can achieve your potential.

You don't want to die with your full potential still within you.

> "Don't die with your music still in you."
> –Wayne Dyer

You can design a life that allows you to maximize your full potential.

Questions to Ponder:

1. Do I like the image that I hold of myself right now?
2. What negative labels have I inherited that no longer serve me?
3. How could I redesign an image of myself that would make me feel fully alive?
4. Who are my current role models? Why? What do I want to harvest from them?
5. What would be the impact on the other parts of my arena if I shift my negative labels to positive labels?

Guideposts to Designing Your Self-Image:

GUIDEPOST #1: Look for role models of women you admire.

- Study women you admire and observe how you can apply the skills they have acquired. Learn from them. You can become a walking student of other women's lives.
- Any time you feel tempted to compare yourself, celebrate the good in others and then harvest.
- Role models are not always easy to find but they can help you break free from your limitations.

GUIDEPOST #2: You are not stuck.

- You can design and redesign yourself over and over again. Every season requires a new design for your life.
- If you feel stuck, invest in a coach or training program to help you get unstuck.

GUIDEPOST #3: You will always have critics.

- Chances are, your critics are not in the arena of their own life. They cannot fight your war if they have ignored their interior battles. You have to settle into the reality that they will always be there.
- Don't fight critics, learn from them.
- When I first started The Woman School, I lost a dear friend who I thought would be there to support me through a vulnerable season of my life. It was the most heart-wrenching pain I have ever endured from a close friend. She blatantly criticized me on a Facebook post, and it sent shock waves to my system. She called me prideful for posting blogs about myself. She hurt me because I am fiercely loyal, and her criticism cut deep. Critics cut deep, but I have learned to harvest from my critics.

GUIDEPOST #4: Write "I Am" Statements and Rewire them Daily.

- Use the Rewire Formula on the following page to help you design a new self-image.

- To replace your self-image, write a script that you will repeat daily to help you create neural connections.

- At the same time, acquire new skills to help you achieve the self-image design that you want.

Figure 5.7

REWIRE FORMULA : WR3

Write — Write your "I am" Statement daily.

Recite — Recite your statements many times a day.

Repeat — Repeat the process of writing and reciting daily.

Retreat — Retreat into your imagination and imagine the impact.

Go to redefinesuccessforwomen.com for a free printable download.

WR3 REWIRE FORMULA

W	WRITE	Write your "I am" statements daily. Write them out five times a day for thirty days.
R	RECITE	Recite your statements many times a day. Recite them when you wake up, at midday, and the end of the day. The more you say them, the quicker they are wired into your brain. Memorize your "I am" statements.
R	REPEAT	Repeat the process of writing and reciting daily. Keep a journal on your nightstand so you can write in the morning and before you go to bed. It should take less than a minute. You could also use your phone alarm to remind you to recite them a few times a day.
R	RETREAT	Retreat into your imagination and imagine the impact. This is an important step. Your imagination is a powerful force to help you fight for what you want. Imagine the impact of the new self-image you want and allow your thoughts to move you emotionally.

Now, you are ready! Download the worksheet below and design your new self-image.

Figure 5.8

SELF-IMAGE ARENA

Using the Guidepost, how do you want to design or redesign your Self-Image Arena in a way that fulfills you?

UNIVERSAL DESIRE	UNIQUE DESIGN	SKILLS & STRATEGIES	IMPACT	ROLE MODEL
Confident Full Potential	Write down how you want to design your self-image.	What skills and strategies can you think of that will help you achive what you want?	How will this new design impact every other part of your arena?	Who are your role models and what can you harvest from them?

Go to redefinesuccessforwomen.com for a free printable download.

HEALTH: The integration of your mental, emotional, physical, and spiritual health that leads to optimal energy for contribution.

Figure 5.9

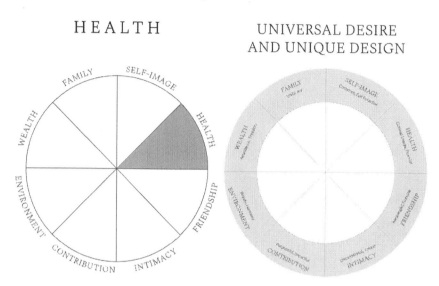

A caveat: Some of us have real limitations that make it extremely challenging to have optimal health. The goal here is learning how to manage our minds so we can attain and maintain peace, regardless of the unknown circumstances that come our way. Now, there are real tragedies in life that make this part of the arena an uphill battle but regardless of the challenge, we can choose to find peace.

Regardless of external circumstances that are beyond our control, we deeply desire to be healthy. Who would not want optimal energy?

I am constantly talking to my children about how to manage their health and the purpose of integrated health. What good is eating an organic diet and exercising every day if we don't know how to manage our minds and become steeped in anxiety?

I find it counterproductive to talk about exercise and nutrition void of mind management and emotional command. I also think it is equally counterproductive to talk about strength and resilience without talking about the importance of taking care of our physical health. I believe in integrated health.

What does it mean to be healthy? There are many different ways to look at this, so I am going to give you the simple version of how we describe health in The Woman School.

- Mental: Our thoughts
- Emotional: How we feel
- Physical: Our bodies
- Spiritual: Our spirit

Your thoughts impact your emotions which impact your physiology which impacts your spiritual receptivity.

If you ruminate on negative thoughts, you start to feel anxious. This impacts your physical body and your spirit. Every part of you impacts the other and seeing your life with eyes of wholeness is crucial for your fulfillment.

In the health arena, you will want to pay attention to your mental, emotional, physical, and spiritual health and create an integrated design.

Align your Design with the Universal Desire: Optimal Energy

Optimal Energy means that you have an abundance of energy for contribution. You don't want to be in perpetual exhaustion. You don't want to be too tired to live your moments. You want to be ready to give the best of who you are to those around you.

Align your Design with the Universal Desire: Peace

You want a life that brings harmony to your soul. There is peace when your heart feels safe. If you are not in command of your emotions, then your days will feel like a volatile roller coaster. What you want is to be a steady pillar of reliance, strong enough to interiorly manage external circumstances you cannot control.

Questions to Ponder:

1. How would you currently describe your mental health?
2. How is your current mental and emotional health affecting your body and your spirit?
3. Who are some of the most resilient and peaceful women you know? Would they be good role models in this arena?
4. What are some of the physical roadblocks that are inhibiting you from optimal energy?
5. What strategies could you implement to help create optimal energy?

Guideposts to Designing Your Health:

GUIDEPOST #1: Take an inventory of your thoughts.

- Your thoughts are so powerful. They impact your emotions and the quality of your day. Replace negative thoughts that no longer serve you.
- You become what you think about, so think about the life you want instead of the life you don't want.
  - Replace: "This is so horrible..." with "I learned from it."
  - Replace: "I can't stand that person..." with "I won't let that person rob me of my day."

GUIDEPOST #2: Manage your words.

- Your words have power. Your words create images in your brain and they shape your perception of life. The words you choose create images in your brain and activate your Reticular Activating System.

- If I tell you to think of a refrigerator, what comes to mind? A fridge.

    - If I tell you to think of a blrdkght, what comes to mind? Nothing, because this word has no meaning in your brain.
    - If I ask you to imagine a woman who is stressed, you can see a disheveled woman who is tired.

- Your words can drain you or bring more life into your life, so be mindful. Choose words that help you achieve the life you want.
- Change your words, change your perspective. Download our "Illegal Words" guide. Identify any words you want to make illegal for yourself.

Figure 5.10

ILLEGAL WORDS
CHANGE YOUR WORDS, CHANGE YOUR PERSPECTIVE

Horrible	It was not the best
Overwhelming	A bit of a dance, in transition
Curse word	Sugar plum macaroni hotdog
Awful	Interesting
Exhausting	I could use a break
So bad	Lots to learn from it
Draining	It robbed me of my energy
Stress	Time to recalibrate
Anxious	I'm doing the dance
Dumb	Not the best choice
Stupid	Not the best choice
Shut up	Please be quiet
Hate	I dislike it
Annoying	You are frustrating me
Weird	Interesting, different
Lazy	Not being proactive
Negative Labels	This behavior needs recalibration
Liar	Dishonest

Go to redefinesuccessforwomen.com for a free printable download.

GUIDEPOST #3: How you treat your body has a cause and effect.

- What you eat matters. It affects how you feel so you need to pay attention to what you consume.
    - When my kids eat sugar, they turn into dramatic human beings who can't seem to speak in reasonable sentences.
    - I have a long family history of diabetes, so when I eat rice, it turns to sugar and my brain feels like mush.
- Our bodies are uniquely created so outside stimuli impacts each person differently. Pay attention to how specific foods impact your overall health.

GUIDEPOST #4: Learn kitchen skills.

- Learning to cook a simple nutritious meal and being competent in cleaning a kitchen quickly and efficiently avoids:

    - Buying fast food
    - Becoming a victim to stress that arises from a dirty kitchen
    - Worrying about how to feed your family
    - Dreading cooking because of the time it takes to cook and clean
- If you want to honor your body as a sacred temple, you need to nourish yourself with quality food.
- To avoid overwhelm, learn basic kitchen skills to help you make quality food choices.

GUIDEPOST #4: Make time for silence.

- Mediation, prayer, and spending time in silence are non-negotiable practices for optimal health. There is plenty of proven data to show the positive impact of meditation on overall health. Without giving yourself space to grow spiritually, it is challenging to optimize your energy.
- Make time to prepare yourself for the day before you are shoved into your morning.
- Take time to invest in knowing why you were created by the Creator, so you can fulfill your unique purpose.

Now, you are ready! Download the worksheet below and design your new self-image.

Figure 5.11

HEALTH ARENA

Using the Guidepost, how do you want to design or redesign your Health Arena in a way that fulfills you?

UNIVERSAL DESIRE	UNIQUE DESIGN	SKILLS & STRATEGIES	IMPACT	ROLE MODEL
Optimal Energy Peaceful	Write down how you want to design your health.	What skills and strategies can you think of that will help you achieve what you want?	How will this new design impact every other part of your arena?	Who are your role models and what can you harvest from them?

Go to redefinesuccessforwomen.com for a free printable download.

FRIENDSHIP: Accompaniment and accountability in the journey to becoming your highest and best self.

Figure 5.12

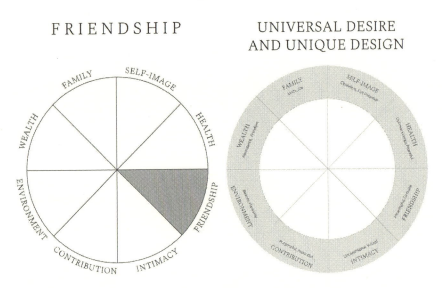

Did you know that loneliness has been declared an epidemic?

How is it possible for us to live in a hyper-connected world yet suffer from a loneliness epidemic?

Can we get to the root of this problem?
Or do we accept that this is the way the world is—that loneliness is now the norm?

How is it that you can go to a party for four hours and interact with people yet still feel empty when you leave? Yet some women can have a fifteen-minute conversation with a friend and feel deeply nurtured.

What is the difference?

Depth. We want deep meaningful conversations that inspire us to think deeper about our lives.

I do not believe that loneliness is an isolation problem but rather a communication crisis.

If we learned better communication skills and acquired skills to create healthy friendships, then we would be less at risk for loneliness.

I believe the loneliness crisis could be remedied if we could learn effective communication skills, boundaries, setting expectations, and a few more that would significantly change the way that we qualify friendship.

We need friends who help satisfy our thirst for depth and meaning, but we can only achieve that if we have the skills necessary for quality friendships.

The purpose of friendship is to accompany each other along the journey of life's ups and downs and hold us accountable to becoming our highest and best self. Everything else is secondary to this primary purpose.

Of course, we want to enjoy our friends, but when we feel nurtured, we enjoy each other even more.

If our friendships do not challenge us to be better, then we risk burying our potential simply because we lack the necessary infrastructure to push and challenge us to maximize our potential.

You are the average of the five people you hang out with most.

- If your circle of friends are insincere, you are at risk of becoming insincere.

- If your circle of friends are steeped in negativity and gossip, you risk becoming negative.
- If your circle of friends have made comparison a norm, then you risk feeling insecure.
- If your inner circle of friends are not intentional about designing a life of wholeness, you risk compromising parts of who you are.
- If your inner circle of friends are dreaming, designing their lives, and personally developing themselves, then your friendships will be fulfilling.
- The quality of your friends impacts the quality of your life.

There are three types of friendship that we talk about at The Woman School:

1. Mentee Friendship: Friends we often have to lead.
2. Mentor Friendship: Friends from whom we often harvest wisdom.
3. Mutual Friendship: Friends who allow for mutual growth and development.

The reason for bringing clarity to different types of friendships is to have proper expectations of our friends, and not expect something from them that they are not capable of giving. Otherwise, we grow in resentment. We want to give from a place of generosity and not resentment.

To be fulfilled, we have to be intentional about designing friendships that meet our needs for genuine connection.

Align your Design with the Universal Desire: Meaning

You don't want shallow friends who leave you empty after a conversation. It is a waste of time and energy. You want to find friends who seek meaning and connection.

Align your Design with the Universal Desire: Genuine

You can feel when someone is insincere. You feel used and devalued. Being genuine means there is a congruence between what you are thinking and how you are acting toward a person. If you want to be fulfilled, then choose friends who are genuine.

Questions to Ponder:

1. Are the current friendships that I am surrounding myself with bringing meaning to my life?
2. Do I struggle with comparison and unhealthy competition with my friends? Why or why not?
3. What are the qualities in friendships that would help me pursue my dreams?
4. What kind of friend am I? What kind of friend do I want to be?
5. What are some boundaries I need to create with some of my friendships?

Guideposts for Designing Friendship:

GUIDEPOST #1: You need a standard for friendship.

- You need to write down what you want in a friend and what your non-negotiables are, so you can hold yourself accountable to your standard. There is a decline in quality friendships for multiple reasons but one is that our friendships are void of standards. Standards hold us accountable for how we show up. We can't just do whatever we want to our friends and expect to have quality friends. For example, women who value their worth will not tolerate toxic conversations.
- Download the worksheet below to process and design the type of friendships you desire.

Figure 5.13

CREATING A STANDARD FOR FRIENDSHIP

I DON'T WANT TO PUT UP WITH FRIENDS WHO ARE:	WHAT I LOOK FOR IN FRIENDSHIPS ARE:	MY STANDARD: WHAT I BELIEVE I DESERVE AS A FRIEND
LIST 5 OF YOUR CLOSEST FRIENDS	LIST FRIENDS THAT NEED BOUNDARIES	WHAT MAKES YOU A GOOD FRIEND?

Go to redefinesuccessforwomen.com for a free printable download.

GUIDEPOST #2: You cannot give what you do not have.

- If you want good friends then you have to be a good friend first. You cannot expect something from someone that you have not first expected from yourself.
- Learn how to be a friend, how to be sincere, and how to bring meaning to your conversations and connections. The way to do this is by building skill after skill. The quality of

your friendships hinges on your ability to *skill-up*; the more skilled you are, the more fulfilling your friendships can be.
- What are some of the key skills you need to find quality friends?
- Rate your skill level below and you will see the direct connection between quality friendships and your skill level.
- If you feel skill deprived, don't be discouraged! You can *skill-up* and find what you are looking for.

Rate yourself 1 - 10, "10" being super skilled and "0" being skilled deprived.

Conversation skills	
Asking quality questions	
Listening intently (7% words, 38% tonality, and 55% body language)	
Communicating your boundaries effectively	
Sincerity and seeking the good	
Being a woman of your word	
Respecting boundaries	
Complimenting and celebrating (opposite of comparison)	

GUIDEPOST #3: Use your Reticular Activating System to find the friends you want.

- Write down what you are looking for in a friend and start developing your skills to be the kind of friend you want to find.
- Be patient. Trust that as you grow in awareness, you will start to see what you are looking for.

GUIDEPOST #4: Focus on quality time, not the quantity of time.
- Time is so important and we have very little time in a busy world. Instead of getting upset because of the lack of quantity of time, focus on quality connections that are not bound by time alone.
- Master skills that help you dig deep in the limited time that you have.
- Quality over quantity brings a deeper fulfillment.

GUIDEPOST #5: Friends come in seasons so we have to stay detached.

- I used to get upset when friends seemed to move on from our friendship until I realized that life is full of transitions. I can't hold on to people if I want what is best for them, because what might be best for them is to grow out of our friendship.
- Learn the skill of healthy attachment. It is never easy to grow out of relationships but that is part of the seasons of life. We are all on a journey and sometimes, we have to go our separate ways.
- Instead of harboring resentment, celebrate the gifts that our friends gave us during a specific season. When you can be grateful for the season that you have, then you don't have to harbor a grudge, you are free to celebrate them.
- Harness what you have gained during your time together and carry it to new friendships.

Now, you are ready! Download the worksheet below and design your Friendship Arena.

Figure 5.14

FRIENDSHIP ARENA

Using the Guidepost, how do you want to design or redesign your Friendship Arena in a way that fulfills you?

UNIVERSAL DESIRE	UNIQUE DESIGN	SKILLS & STRATEGIES	IMPACT	ROLE MODEL
Meaningful Genuine	Write down how you want to design your friendships.	What skills and strategies can you think of that will help you achieve what you want?	How will this new design impact every other part of your arena?	Who are your role models and what can you harvest from them?

Go to redefinesuccessforwomen.com for a free printable download.

INTIMACY ARENA: A sacred space reserved for someone who has earned the right to share in the most tender and vulnerable parts of who we are.

Figure 5.15

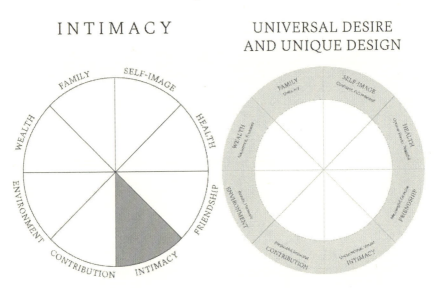

Intimacy has to be reserved only for someone who has earned the right to share in the most vulnerable and tender parts of who we are. We are created to love and be loved and finding that significant someone who can fulfill our need for intimacy is beautiful.

I was so afraid of dating. I was afraid that I would end up with a man who would not value me.

After I finally figured out what I wanted in a relationship, the problem remained that I did not have the skills to get what I wanted. So, for five years, I was very intentional about cultivating new skills for deep intimacy. I had to work through deep wounds but it was worth it to have a man like Ryan.

We have shared sixteen years of a beautiful marriage. We have our difficult moments but our intimacy keeps getting stronger each year. We love the privilege of building a business together while raising our eight children. There is no secret to a beautiful marriage—you have to *Train-Up* and grow together. Our marriage gets better because we have intentionally created a culture that prioritizes self-development.

You have to protect the most sacred part of who you are. You cannot squander your heart and expect to be fulfilled. You have a duty to grow so you can give more of yourself to the relationship. And it is so worth it.

Yes, relationships can have challenging moments but how many of our challenges stem from our lack of skills?

Sadly, there is no training on how to protect your sacred space and how to prepare someone to enter this space. Regardless of what your intimate relationship looks like right now or in the past, have hope! If you are willing to *Train-Up*, things can be better.

Align your Design with the Universal Desire: Unconditional

"I love you only if and when you are skinny."
"I love you only if and when you can keep the house clean."

You don't want an intimate relationship that places conditions on love. You are going to make mistakes and you need to know that you remain worthy of love, even when you are not so lovable.

The most sacred parts of who you are have different rules from other relationships because you reveal parts of yourself that you protect from other people. You need a standard that is based on trust.

In order to have a strong relationship, love needs to be unconditional.

Align your Design with the Universal Desire: Valued

Who wants to be taken for granted? We have a universal desire to feel significant, especially by those we value most.

Regardless of where your relationship stands at the moment, there is no denying that you are valuable and deserve to be appreciated, honored, and loved fully.

The problem is, people who fall into the trap of toxic relationships usually have an inability to value themselves first.

You deserve to feel valued as you are.

Questions to Ponder:

1. Do I feel admired by my significant other? Why or why not?
2. Do I feel like my relationship is getting better or worse each year? Why?
3. Do I have any unhealed wounds that are holding me back from the relationship that I want?
4. Are there any unmet needs in my relationship? Describe how this is hurting me.
5. What new strategies can I implement that would make my intimate relationship grow stronger?

Guideposts for Designing Intimacy:

GUIDEPOST #1: You deserve to be admired.

- This is one of the hardest concepts that I teach. It is hard because women have been so devalued that the idea that they are made for admiration seems foreign. Ask yourself, *If I could, would I want to be admired by the man you admire*

most? If it is taking you longer to answer a resounding "yes," then there could be a wound of admiration that hurts you without you even knowing.
- Women often don't consider admiration because they have settled for scraps. To admire someone means that you are in awe of who they are because their presence has left a profound impression on your life. If admiration means that they are in awe of your goodness, then why should you not desire it?
- The reason women don't aspire for admiration is that they feel undeserving of it. Yet our hearts soften at the idea that who we are is so valuable that we are worthy of deep awe. This is what we want.
- Let me explain the Metric of Lovability:
    - Appreciation-They see you.
    - Acknowledge-They not only see you, but they also acknowledge your value.
    - Affirmation-They don't only see and hear you, but they affirm the good in you.
    - Affection-They see you, hear you, and seek the good in you which is why they desire to be around you.
    - Admiration-They see you, hear you, see the good in you, and want to be around you because who you are leaves such a profound impression that they are in awe of you. Your presence inspires them.
- Ask yourself, *Do I feel admired by my significant someone? Why or Why not?*
- Design a life in which you are deeply admired in the most intimate parts of who you are.

Figure 5.16

METRIC OF LOVABILITY
DEVALUED ⟶ VALUED

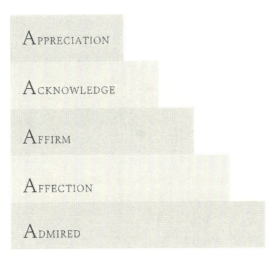

Go to redefinesuccessforwomen.com for a free printable download.

GUIDEPOST #2: You can't change anyone.

- You can't change anyone, you can only inspire them to change for themselves. When we launched The Woman School, very quickly women asked, "How can I change my man?" My response is that you can't. The harsh reality is that you can lead a horse to the water, but you cannot make it drink.
- No one wants to be coerced into a change they have not initiated for themselves. We have to stop this false agenda of expecting people to change—it it not worth the fight.
- What you can do is transform yourself from within so that you become an inspiration to your significant someone. When your life becomes full of light, it inspires others, and that is how you can invite someone to change their life.

- At the end of the day, you can't control how your significant someone is going to respond, but you will have a greater chance of them changing by becoming an inspiration first.
- Use the "I3 Formula: Invest, Inspire, Invite" to remind yourself that you can't change anyone without first inspiring them. Invest in yourself first so you can inspire others, and only then can you invite them to do their own interior work.

Figure 5.17

I3 FORMULA

I3 Invest
Inspire
Invite

Go to redefinesuccessforwomen.com for a free printable download.

The Man School began as a direct fruit of women asking for mindset and skill set training for the men in their lives—their husbands, fathers, sons, and co-workers. If you want to learn more about The Man School Training, go to thewholenessschool.com.

GUIDEPOST #3: Lack of accountability creates monsters around us and within us.

- When you don't hold your significant other to a high standard, then you give them permission to be a lesser version of themselves, making room for them to become entitled.
- At the same time, you can create a monster within you because you grow in resentment when parts of yourself are not being honored.

- Holding your significant someone accountable is a form of contribution. But not everyone knows how to receive accountability, especially if they are accustomed to no accountability. If someone is not open to growing, holding them accountable will be met with resistance. You cannot control how they respond, but you can control how you respond. Holding someone accountable is a pivotal skill that helps you protect your life of wholeness.

Now, you are ready! Download the worksheet below and design your Intimacy Arena.

Figure 5.18

INTIMACY ARENA

Using the Guidepost, how do you want to design or redesign your Intimacy Arena in a way that fulfills you?

UNIVERSAL DESIRE	UNIQUE DESIGN	SKILLS & STRATEGIES	IMPACT	ROLE MODEL
Unconditional, Valued	Write down how you want to design your intimacy.	What skills and strategies can you think of that will help you achieve what you want?	How will this new design impact every other part of your arena?	Who are your role models and what can you harvest from them?

Go to redefinesuccessforwomen.com for a free printable download

CONTRIBUTION ARENA: Your ability to contribute your unique purpose in a specific season of your life.

Figure 5.19

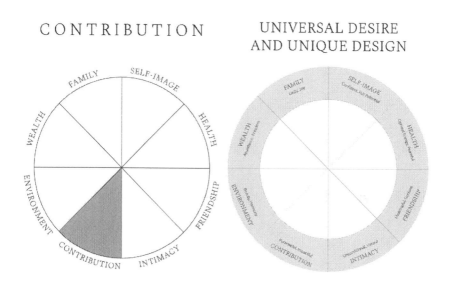

When we think of contribution, we automatically think big, macro, and huge.

In contrast, what I am proposing here is contribution as a way of life. We are made for contribution; giving fulfills us.

Even your smile could be the contribution someone needs to affirm their value. Contribution is about making others feel valuable.

The more you train yourself in emotional intelligence, asking quality questions, empathy, and listening, the greater you are able to contribute in both the micro and macro moments of your day.

Contribution is also about using your talent for good. It is about finding work that you love while being a light to those around you.

Your contribution is unique to your specific season of life. In order to be fulfilled in this arena, you have to pay attention to the different roles you are currently playing.

Ask yourself, *How am I bringing value to others through the current roles I am in?*

We are each called to greatness. Greatness is fulfilling your unique and irreplaceable purpose in this world. In this arena, I suggest that you aim to create a lifestyle in which you are living your ordinary moments in an extraordinary way as a way of contributing to the people around you.

Align your Design with the Universal Desire: Purposeful

Your fulfillment cannot be void of your irreplaceable purpose. This is why you can't just do whatever you want to do; you have to do what is in harmony with who you were fashioned to be. You can't be fulfilled outside of your purpose. You are uniquely made for your purpose.

Align your Design with the Universal Desire: Impactful

You want to know your existence is valued because you are creating a positive impact. To be fulfilled, you must be convicted of your irreplaceable contribution right now.

Questions to Ponder:

1. Do I feel like I am doing work that fulfills my purpose? Why or why not?
2. What work would I love to do if there were no obstacles?
3. Am I currently in an unhealthy toxic work environment? Why?
4. When I look back on my life, how would I like to remember it?
5. What is my current dream of the season?

Guideposts for Designing Contribution:

GUIDEPOST #1: Your contribution is unique to you.

- No one else can offer what you offer to the world. It is yours alone to give.
- If you decide not to *Train-Up*, you will feel the burden of wasting your time and potential. It will feel a lot like restlessness which eventually leads to anxiety. If you are unwilling to do your part to offer your irreplaceable contribution right now, then there will be a hole in the tapestry of life, for no one can offer what you offer.

GUIDEPOST #2: Find work that you love.

- Whether you are paid for it or not, find work that you love to do because doing that you love fuels you to do great work. You have to find something you are passionate about. For example, when I started The Woman School, long before I built a business around it, I trained women for free because I was passionate about helping women design a life that was whole. My passion was fueled by the pain I saw in women's eyes.
- Simon Sinek reminds us, "Working hard for something we don't care about is called stress. Working hard for something we love is called passion." Just because we are passionate about the work we do, does not mean there will not be challenging moments, but it does mean that we have a greater capacity to endure hardship.
- Steve Jobs said, "The only way to do great work is to love what you do. If you haven't found it yet, keep looking. Don't settle. As with all matters of the heart, you'll know when you find it."
    - You will know when you find it. It will be revealed to you with each step you take.

GUIDEPOST #3: There are three types of contribution and each is equally important.

- #1 CONTRIBUTION IN THE MOMENT. Every moment, you have the ability to create a positive impact through your encounters. Though seemingly insignificant, they can create a ripple effect that you might not even know. Imagine becoming so skilled in creating opportunities to contribute to the present moment. A heartfelt smile at the grocery store could change someone's day. What you offer in the present is a gift. You can rest each night knowing that you have done your part to make this world a little bit better.
- #2 CONTRIBUTION OF THE SEASON. Life is made up of seasons and every season has a unique and irreplaceable contribution that you are destined to fulfill. Just like the seasons come and go, your life also has seasons: a new job, a newlywed, a new mom, or an empty nester. Your contribution is unique with every season. If you are a new mom, you have something important to offer the world. If you are a college student, you can impact significant change around you, and so on. In this very moment in time, you have a set of people around you that you have been ordained to inspire. No one can offer what you offer. You alone hold the key to your contribution of the season.
- #3 CONTRIBUTION BY LEGACY: At this very moment, you are crafting the legacy that you are leaving through the compounding contribution you are leaving with each and every season. You get to choose your legacy. You can design and redesign how you want your life to be remembered by those who know you. Your life will pass but the impact of your legacy can live in the hearts of many people. When you make it your intention to build a legacy that inspires others to be better, you will live each day in a very fulfilling way.

Now, you are ready! Download the worksheet below and design your Contribution Arena.

Figure 5.20

CONTRIBUTION ARENA

Using the Guidepost, how do you want to design or redesign your Contribution Arena in a way that fulfills you?

UNIVERSAL DESIRE	UNIQUE DESIGN	SKILLS & STRATEGIES	IMPACT	ROLE MODEL
Purposeful Impactful	Write down how you want to design your contribution.	What skills and strategies can you think of that will help you achieve what you want?	How will this new design impact every other part of your arena?	Who are your role models and what can you harvest from them?

Go to redefinesuccessforwomen.com for a free printable download.

ENVIRONMENT ARENA: The exterior space composed of people and culture that impacts your interior life.

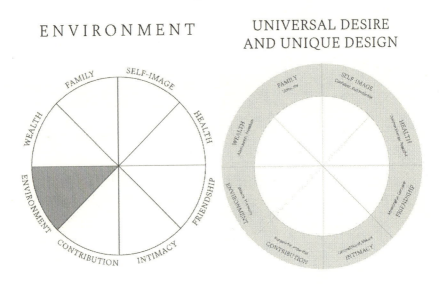

Figure 5.21

Too often, we hear things like...
"I hate going home, it is such a mess."
"Work is so toxic, but I don't have any other choice."
"I don't like being home, it is crazy and chaotic."

Today, women have very little time and training on how to manage their homes, workplaces, and communities. Everything can feel overwhelming and daunting if we've been deprived of the most basic skills necessary to take responsibility for our external environment.

It is a challenge to constantly hold my children to the standard of doing their part to help at home. Like most moms, I sound like a broken record. But I am determined to have them "graduate" from the house knowing how to take responsibility for their environment.

We need to train ourselves to be stewards of our environment. We want a place where we can rest and experience beauty. It doesn't have anything to do with being fancy, but rather, being intentional about creating a beautiful environment with what you have and being grateful for it.

Align your Design with the Universal Desire: Beauty

I am not talking about perfection, but rather, inspiration. When our environment is beautiful, it inspires us to create and expand. A beautiful environment is like a lush garden, full of things that nourish us.

When I was single and working with my mentor, she gave me homework for my environment. It was to design my room to be a place where I wanted to be. There was just one problem...I did not have any money to buy nice things. Even so, Elena challenged me to be creative and resourceful. I went to the local thrift shop and decorated my whole room, and was able to spend very little. It was simple but beautiful. I would go to the local farmers market at the end of the day and ask for any leftover flowers that they were going to throw away, so I always had fresh flowers on my desk. I loved my little beat-up studio basement apartment. It was home to me.

Having nice things can certainly help create a beautiful environment, but I've been in plenty of spaces that looked nice but lacked warmth. In my opinion, what makes an environment beautiful and inviting is when it cultivates a culture of warmth, growth, and joy. You can design your environment in such a way that it fulfills you as well as those who pass through.

Align your Design with the Universal Desire: Harmony

When I think of harmony I think of symphony instruments working together to produce beautiful music. This requires order. Similarly, there must be order in our environment to preserve harmony.

Otherwise, it could feel like anarchy.

- If your child lacks discipline, it throws off the environment.
- If you lack the training to be efficient with cleaning the kitchen and everyone is yelling while cleaning, it makes for a stressful environment.
- If you have a toxic coworker, it will be like a rotten egg whose smell you can't get out of the room.

The tricky part about harmony is that it requires constant work and vigilance. You have to pay attention to the integration of the different parts of your environment, in the same way, that a composer pays attention to the different instruments working together to produce beautiful music. If just one instrument is off-tempo, it throws everyone else off.

Questions to Ponder:

1. Does my current environment inspire me? Why or why not?
2. How do I want to feel in my home?
3. How does the current state of my home make me feel? How does it make my other family members feel?
4. What strategies could I implement that would improve the quality of my home life?
5. What do I need to change about myself in order to improve my home?

Guideposts for Designing Your Environment:

GUIDEPOST #1: Your attitude impacts your environment.

- Your attitude is the combination of your thoughts, feelings, and behavior. How you show up in your environment impacts the quality of your environment. I have pre-teens

and when they come down for breakfast in a crabby mood (we have a No Sleeping-In Standard), I send them back upstairs to recalibrate. My script is, "Please recalibrate sweetie, you don't want to victimize everyone with your crapitude. Come down when you are ready." When they come back down, they are a different person.
- We can't victimize everyone else just because we don't feel well. We can learn to have command of our thoughts and emotions so we can be mindful of how we treat people. It is normal to not feel good at times, and we can give ourselves permission to recalibrate and rest so we don't rob others of their joy.
    - Your attitude is your choice. If you want to design a fulfilling life, you have to take responsibility for your attitude.

GUIDEPOST #2: Your external environment impacts your internal environment.

- Your interior life is composed of your thoughts and emotions. Your interior life determines the quality of your life. But if your exterior environment is toxic, you risk having your interior life being volatile.
- If your work environment is stressful, it will bleed into your home environment whether you like it or not. It is hard to separate parts of yourself, because you are integrated. You have to make tough decisions and create firm boundaries to protect your interior life from toxic environments.
- At the same time, if your interior life is full of chaos, it will negatively impact your exterior environment. Paying attention to the relationship between your exterior world and interior world is an important responsibility, and is crucial for your fulfillment.

GUIDEPOST #3: You have the capacity to impact every room you walk into.

- Think about the many rooms you have walked into throughout your life. Do you remember your first day of high school? Your first date? Your first presentation at work? Every day that you walk into work or every morning that you show up in your kitchen, in every room that you walk into, you have the capacity to create an impact in that room. Maybe it will be through a smile, a hug, a meaningful question, a deep conversation, or listening intently. Maybe it will be through your laughter or your positive presence.
- You walk into so many rooms in your lifetime. Find an opportunity to bring light into that room. The more skills you have, the more strategic you can be about how you impact the room.
- When you live your life looking for opportunities to serve the room, each day will be fulfilling.

Now, you are ready! Download the following worksheet and design your Environment.

Figure 5.22

ENVIRONMENT ARENA

Using the Guidepost, how do you want to design or redesign your Environment Arena in a way that fulfills you?

UNIVERSAL DESIRE	UNIQUE DESIGN	SKILLS & STRATEGIES	IMPACT	ROLE MODEL
Beauty Harmony	Write down how you want to design your environment.	What skills and strategies can you think of that will help you achieve what you want?	How will this new design impact every other part of your arena?	Who are your role models and what can you harvest from them?

Go to redefinesuccessforwomen.com for a free printable download.

WEALTH ARENA: An abundance of time, treasure, and talent for the purpose of contribution.

Figure 5.23

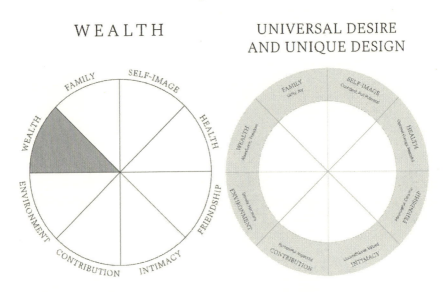

Often, people have strong opinions about wealth...
"Money is evil."
"Rich people are materialistic and greedy."
"I am broke."

Wealth is a hot topic.

There are many different and colliding perspectives that usually stem from our family of origin. Opposing beliefs about money cause division in families and in the workplace.

Rarely are we taught to have an ordered understanding of wealth, yet our ability to manage time and resources impacts every part of our arena.

If you are going to design a wealth arena that fulfills you, then you have to know the purpose of wealth. Wealth is about having an abundance mindset. Abundance, as we define it, is being in a state of gratitude and generosity.

Wealth does not mean millions and millions of dollars. Wealth is simply a mindset—an abundance of time, treasure, and talent that gives you the freedom to be generous.

Wealth is about gratitude and generosity.
When you are grateful, you feel abundant.
When you are generous, you feel abundant.
When you feel like you are able to use your time and talent, you feel abundant.

When you feel like you can give a few extra dollars to organizations you support or help fund your children's piano lessons, you feel abundant.

The goal is to create wealth that makes you feel like you have more than enough.

Gratitude is having a grateful heart. It means that no matter how much you have or don't have, you are grateful. You can't complain and be grateful at the same time. Being fulfilled means that you see your life as half full, not half empty.

Generosity is having a heart for contribution. When you are giving from a full cup, you feel a sense of satisfaction when you know that you are doing something good with your life. You know what makes you happy is not what you have but rather, becoming a vessel for the good.

> "The secret to living is giving." -Tony Robbins

Wealth cannot be limited to money alone. Not everyone is called to create an abundance of wealth.

Maybe your generosity lies in your ability to volunteer your time. Perhaps you have a talent for singing and that is your way of generosity.

An ordered wealth arena can do so much good when it is aligned with your purpose.

Align your Design with the Universal Desire: Abundance

The only reason we don't want abundance is either that we don't know how to achieve it or we feel unworthy of it.

Abundance means that there is an overflow; there is more than enough to fill our cup and the cups of those around us.

Scarcity is the opposite of abundance. When we live in a scarcity mindset, we lean toward fear and lack. We do not trust that we will have more than what we need.

If you use your Reticular Activating System to see scarcity or abundance, that is what you will find, so you might as well focus on what gives you a greater capacity for generosity.

Align your Design with the Universal Desire: Freedom

I remember the first time I heard Grant Cardone say, "Money gives you choices." I had to wrestle with his words because I didn't believe them, but honestly, deep down inside I wished I did.

I didn't want to want wealth, not because I didn't want it, but because I was afraid of it. At that time, I assumed that wealth would make me greedy. This was a limiting belief. Wealth does not make you greedy—you can be greedy regardless of whether you have money or not. People with values use their wealth in valuable ways.

Questions to Ponder:

1. Do I live in an abundance or scarcity mindset? Why?
2. How is my current wealth mindset influencing every other part of my arena?
3. What strategies could I implement that would make me feel wealthier?
4. Am I currently spending abundant amounts of time with the people I love? Why or why not?
5. How would I like to use my wealth?

Guideposts for Designing Wealth:

GUIDEPOST #1: Money can be valuable in the hands of people who have strong values.

- Money is neutral. We can use it for good or for evil. If we teach good people to build wealth, then we can use wealth to bring good and defund evil. There is plenty of evidence that money is used for evil, but the way we can change that is to teach good people to use their money for good.

GUIDEPOST #2: Be proactive about building wealth.

- Money is part of wealth. It gives us resources.
- Instead of waiting for money, find a way to create it.
- Consider investing your time and money to learn how to expand your ability to be more generous.
- Be proactive so you can have reserves to help those around you.

GUIDEPOST #3: Your wealth is not your worth.

- Nothing can change your value. You are not defined by your wealth or your lack of it. Your value does change based on your ability to give back, even though it feels good. Some people might use their wealth to make themselves feel valuable, but this cannot fill the void.
- If you have limiting beliefs regarding wealth, rewire them using neuroplasticity. Rescript old beliefs using our Rewire Formula (refer back figure 5.7 on page 173). Here are some same sample scripts you can use to rewire limiting beliefs around wealth.

  - "Ordered wealth can bring so much good to the world."
  - "People who have strong values use their wealth to bring more value to the world."
  - "My wealth is not my worth."

- If you feel unfulfilled, you can change your belief so that you can see wealth and its higher purpose.
- If you are on the opposite side of the spectrum and are afraid of money, explore role models who use their money for good to help you rewire your limiting beliefs around money.
- Remember that your wealth is not your worth. Your worth is unconditional and cannot be defined by your wealth. Your worth is not for sale, it can never be bought.

Now, you are ready! Download the worksheet below and design your Wealth Arena.

Figure 5.24

WEALTH ARENA

Using the Guidepost, how do you want to design or redesign your Wealth Arena in a way that fulfills you?

UNIVERSAL DESIRE	UNIQUE DESIGN	SKILLS & STRATEGIES	IMPACT	ROLE MODEL
Abundant Freedom	Write down how you want to design your wealth.	What skills and strategies can you think of that will help you achieve what you want?	How will this new design impact every other part of your arena?	Who are your role models and what can you harvest from them?

Go to redefinesuccessforwomen.com for a free printable download.

FAMILY ARENA: The family is the basic unit of society that nurtures our foundation of how we contribute back to society.

Figure 5.25

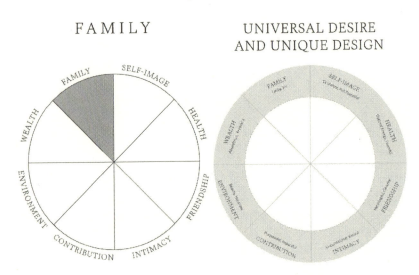

Family is the fabric of society. It is where we come to know ourselves first. It sets the foundation of our perception of how the world works.

My perception of family growing up was that siblings fought like cats and dogs because that was how it was modeled for me by my aunts and uncle. That experience shaped my decision to invest in my friendship with my own brother and sister because I didn't want what I saw. This decision came from my wounds, but I was able to implement an important lesson from witnessing a difficult situation.

No one comes from a perfect family. If you have a family with no drama and have stayed united amidst different beliefs and opinions, consider yourself abnormal.

I believe the family unit is under attack because of how the internet has robbed us of basic communication skills that would benefit our relationships with our siblings and parents. There is a lot of division that arises in a digital world; phones, TV, Music, and video games; our attention is pulled in all directions. What is being normalized for family life is chaos, disrespectful teens, entitled kids, unhappy marriages, and stressful home life. This is not what our hearts long for—we just assume that this must be the only way.

If you are designing a fulfilling life, pay attention to what creates peace and harmony in your family. Be proactive about how you want your family life to be. It is vital to train yourself with the necessary skills so you can preserve your family culture.

Align your Design with the Universal Desire: Unity

There is so much division in families. In general, we don't have a sense of family pride like we used to. For many and varying reasons, we have diluted the need for unity in our homes while promoting world peace. Yet we cannot hope for a peaceful world while our homes are full of anger and hurt. As we know, hurt people hurt other people.

I believe that the most effective way for us to cultivate peace in the world is to be intentional about creating peaceful homes first. It is in the home that we learn how to be united, even among different opinions. That is a skill worthy of mastery in our family dynamics. We need to cultivate wholeness within our family, which requires strategy, training, and a whole lot of discipline.

Align your Design with the Universal Desire: Joy

There is a sign in our living room that reads, "In this home there is joy."

I placed it front and center so we can strategically wire a standard of joy in our home.

Ryan and I are designing a family culture where our children can graduate from our home with a memory of joy. We use wall art as part of our strategy to wire beliefs that one day will serve them. I want them to feel a sense of peace and joy because they know that they are unconditionally loved.

Questions to Ponder:

1. Describe the kind of mother I am now or the kind of mother I want to be. (If you do not aspire to be a mother, you can skip this question.)
2. Is our current family life bringing everyone joy or robbing them of it? Why?
3. Do I instill discipline in my home? Why or why not?
4. What discipline strategy would improve the quality of my home?
5. How could my family members contribute to improving our current family culture?

Guideposts for Designing the Family Arena:

GUIDEPOST #1: An undisciplined life is a hard life. Discipline is key.

- As a mom of eight, discipline is my saving grace. I am committed to raising children who can give themselves a command and follow it (that is how Jim Rohn defines discipline). I want my children to understand that an undisciplined life will make their life hard.
- I have a script book drawer in my kitchen. Each child has their own notebook with their name written on it. When they need to rewire a new habit, belief, or label, I ask them to bring out their script book to help rewire their brain.

Writing scripts is a Donovan norm. My children have written 10, 25, 100, 500, and some up to 1,000 scripts depending on the offense and the age. And they love it! (I'm joking—they dislike it and they resist it.) Even though I've explained the rewiring process of the brain and how the scripts work for them, they resist the habit anyway. But I am okay with that, I would rather them resist me now than resent me later for not helping them develop certain disciplines. Here are some of our house rules in case you want to harvest from them:

- We use scripts to rewire new skills.
- We record ourselves reciting our scripts.
- If children complain, they write a gratitude list in their script book.
- We practice the questions we ask people to make them feel important.
- We set expectations before we go to a party to remind each of us how to present our highest and best self.

- I want my children to know that discipline is necessary to achieve their dreams, so they can design a life that is fulfilling. To me, discipline is my way of contributing to their future.

GUIDEPOST #2: Create a Growth Environment.

- Carol Dweck's book, *Mindset*, helped Ryan and I create the language we needed to raise children who are open to learning and expanding their mindset. Creating a growth environment gives children and parents permission to fail, to learn, and to not feel like they have to be perfect. Creating a growth mindset in families is so important to be open to learning new skills.
- How do we create a growth environment? We make personal development part of our homes.

- I had one month to write this book, so I pulled long hours with late nights and early mornings, just so I could reach my deadline. Then after a month of work, I got my transcript from my editor and it was not good at all. A whole month was wasted and all my hard work went down the drain. I decided to start from scratch with only two weeks left to write. I looked at my son with a smile on my face and told him, "This is what it takes to fight for your dreams. When you have given 1000% and it was not enough, you have to push and start over again. That is how we grow. We pick up the pieces of our disappointment, and with gratitude, celebrate another opportunity to fulfill our passions." He is an aspiring golfer, hoping to fulfill his dream to play professional golf. I feel it is in these moments that I am able to model for him what it takes to grow toward your dreams. Mommy needed to model a growth mindset. I had to be willing to fail, rise again, and learn from my mistakes.

GUIDEPOST #3: Create a wholesome life.

- As a young girl in the Philippines, I grew up watching the sunrise and sunset. We went stargazing with friends and family. My uncle played the guitar and we sang and danced. There were no phones to distract us. We enjoyed nature, quality conversations, and great food, and we laughed a lot. When I came to the United States, I saw a lot of binge drinking and my friends got into drugs. This was never a temptation for me because I had experienced a wholesome childhood, in spite of some pain I endured from not having my family. Still, a wholesome life helped fill the void of my parents being gone.
- Today, the word wholesome is not something we often use as a strategy to win our children over against nega-

tive influences, but I think we should. We should offer them quality and rich experiences. We should sell them on laughter and wholesome conversations. They seek lower choices because they don't know how good it can be. It is like tasting quality wine—it is hard to go back after you've tasted the best, and you can recognize when the quality is not there.

- Selling is a non-negotiable skill for mothers. We have to be skilled in selling homework, helping with chores, discipline, and pretty much everything else. They say that selling is the most lucrative profession. I think selling is one of the most important skills we can develop as mothers. As my husband often reminds me, "Selling is not telling, that is repelling. Selling is asking questions." Selling to my children is a skill I need to grow into but I believe that I have a duty to sell to them a wholesome life.

Now, you are ready! Download the following worksheet and design your Family Arena.

Figure 5.26

FAMILY ARENA

Using the Guidepost, how do you want to design or redesign your Family Arena in a way that fulfills you?

UNIVERSAL DESIRE	UNIQUE DESIGN	SKILLS & STRATEGIES	IMPACT	ROLE MODEL
Unity
Joy	Write down how you want to design your family.	What skills and strategies can you think of that will help you achieve what you want?	How will this new design impact every other part of your arena?	Who are your role models and what can you harvest from them?

Go to redefinesuccessforwomen.com for a free printable download.

Fulfillment is Your Choice

Figure 5.4

How do you feel? Was it challenging to go through each arena? Or easy enough?

The Arena exercise above is just the beginning.

Let's recap.

So far I have taken you on a journey to discover how to design a fulfilling life.

- In Chapter 1: We identified our common enemy and gave language to our struggles.

- In Chapter 2: We dug deep and clarified the desires of the heart.
- In Chapter 3: We introduced the *Fulfillment Formula* where I teach the trifecta as a blueprint for a fulfilling life. We clarified the importance of having a dream, a wholeness design, and how to develop ourselves.
- In Chapter 4: We learned how to discover our dreams, the purpose of our dreams, and how to create a plan to fulfill them.
- In Chapter 5: We learned how to design a life of wholeness. I walked you through the arena exercises to help you design an integrated and fulfilling life.
- In Chapter 6: We will clarify what it means to develop ourselves in order to achieve both the dream and the design.
- In Chapter 7: I am going to send you off so you can continue the great work we have begun here together.

At this point, I hope you are convinced that your fulfillment is your choice.

You now have a blueprint to design and redesign your life in every season.

I hope you take the time to ponder what would truly fulfill you in every part of your arena.

My hope for you is that you learn the skill to identify a clear vision of what would make you whole.

Knowing what you want is half the battle. The other half is you taking action.

P̲ause
P̲onder
A̲ct

Chapter 5

1. Describe a whole new version of yourself.
2. How would you redesign every part of your arena to align with your fulfillment?
3. How are you going to invest in your life of wholeness?

CHAPTER 6

SUCCESS REQUIRES YOU TO DESIGN YOU

1. Information is not Formation
2. Success Requires You to Design a Whole New Version of You
3. Your Fulfillment is Your Responsibility, and Discipline is the Secret Sauce
4. *Train-Up* For the Life You Want
5. The Cost of an Underdeveloped Self
6. Rules and Freedom
7. 21 Rules of Being a Woman

Figure 6.1

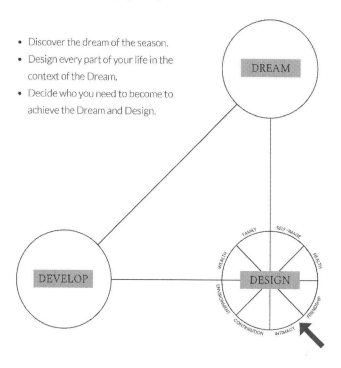

Information is Not Formation

In an information world where we have information that is instantly at our disposal, it is easy to assume information equals transformation.

BUT.

If that were true, it would mean:

- By reading books on how to lose weight you would guarantee your weight loss.
- By inhaling information on how to become an Olympic gymnast, you would be guaranteed the gold medal—even without training.
- By reading 100 books on how to make money, you would be guaranteed to make a million dollars while sitting on the beach.

I wish it was that easy.
I wish I could lose weight by just reading about weight loss.
I wish reading about world-class athletes made me an instant champion.
I wish reading about business would guarantee me millions of dollars.

But it does not.
Knowing does not equal being.

"Knowing" is about acquiring information.
"Being" is about shaping our mindset, developing our skills, and consistently training ourselves so we can take what we know and put it into practice until it becomes part of our being.

Eventually, what we know becomes who we are.

Information alone is not enough to guarantee your transformation. There is a missing link—what we call formation.

Formation is the shaping of your mind, body, and spirit to match your intended design. When a potter has an image of what she wants to create, she carefully shapes her clay to match the design she has envisioned in her mind.

The process of forming the clay is the same process that we go through to align ourselves toward who we want to become; we see it first, then we form it.

Acquiring information does not serve us unless we take action and put what we know into practice.

As a matter of fact, information overload could paralyze us into inaction.

I have a solution to bridge this gap, I call it the Transformation Formula.

The Transformation Formula can hold you accountable for taking massive action.

TRANSFORMATION FORMULA:

Figure 6.2

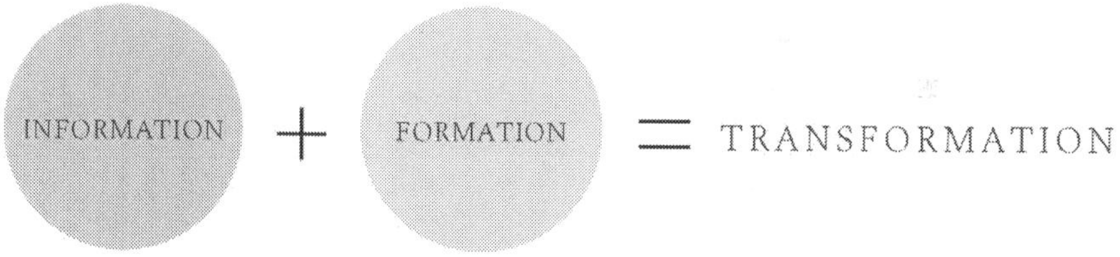

INFORMATION + FORMATION = TRANSFORMATION

You can't sustainably achieve the life that you want by just reading books, listening to podcasts, and going on motivational retreats. You have to *train-up* and expand your mindset and skill set consistently for you to experience exponential growth.

Expanding your mindset will allow you to grow your skill set faster. In business, the more I expand my mindset as well as develop new skills, the faster I can see the transformation in my business. But if

I just read about business without implementing it, that would be my demise.

Most of us have built a habit of acquiring information, but not many of us put that information into actionable training.

This formula *Information + Formation* ought to be the foundation of how you design and develop yourself to achieve the life of wholeness that you want.

You become what you repeatedly do.

Success Requires You to Design a Whole New Version of You

Speaking in public makes me want to barf.

I realize this is not a pleasant visual, but it is honestly the most accurate description of how public speaking makes me feel.

As I was preparing to present on the same stage as John Maxwell and Ed Mylett, I also thought about what I would say when I met them:

- *Should I ask them questions? Do I smile and nod?*
- *Do I tell them about myself?*
- *Do I tell them about my kids—unless they don't like kids?*
- *How should I walk, talk, and breathe? What if I sneeze?*
- *January! What are you doing?*

It was comical.

I was ruminating on strategies of how I wanted to show up for them, which was code for how to "impress" them.

I felt myself sinking into a quicksand of self-doubt.
But for crying out loud, January, you train women against self-doubt!

How did I fall into the trap of having to prove that I was good enough to be on that same stage?

I was vigilant enough to catch my pattern and not spiral down the path of proving and pleasing to feel valued.

I knew what I needed to do because I'd trained women with the exact training I now needed. Information plus formation equals the transformation I needed.

It is usually the case that I give women training on things I need for myself.

So what is that training?

To not feel insecure on that stage, I needed to work on my SELF-IMAGE. I needed to design January Donovan's self-image on that stage. I needed to design January Donovan in my imagination first so I could work backward from that design.

I needed to replace my old self-image of someone who is afraid of speaking (aka barfs when speaking in public), with someone who is passionate and fierce when she speaks, regardless of what people think of her.

I had neurologically wired my self-image as someone afraid of public speaking. This neurological connection that I had wired in my brain had heavily influenced my decisions as a business owner. I was passionate about teaching women, but I always quickly refused any speaking engagements, even though I knew how good it could be for The Woman School brand. My negative self-image impacted the expansion of the business, and it held us back.

But if I want to reach millions of women, I have no choice but to replace my fear of speaking on a stage with a new self-image of a woman who is fierce about speaking because she wants to fight for every woman's value. It is no longer about me. It is about me answering my call to fight for women's worth. I had made speaking only about myself, rather than making myself a means for greater contribution.

I used the rewire formula to create a new self-image of January Donovan as a passionate speaker who was unapologetic about her mission.

This new self-image informed me on which new skills, scripts, and strategies I needed, because designing a new self-image gave me a clear vision of who I wanted to become.

I just had to work backward from that vision.

The best part about designing your self-image is that you can redesign yourself at any moment when the old image no longer serves your highest good. As you grow in deeper awareness, so does your capacity to redesign a new version of yourself.

There is something empowering about having the ability to design yourself and work on the discipline necessary to achieve the design that you want.

Discipline is your superpower.
Discipline is my saving grace.

My self-image as a fierce speaker empowered me to discipline myself to grow new skills. I took a class on speaking, wrote down my speech numerous times, studied brilliant speakers, and imagined myself touching the hearts of women. I knew who I needed to become to serve millions of women—and a life of discipline is what it takes to make it all possible.

Clarity of vision becomes fuel to our discipline.

> "Discipline is giving yourself a command and following it up with action." -Bob Proctor

How do you know what command to give yourself?
It is based on the self-image that you design.

A potter knows how to chisel her clay based on the image of what she wants her clay to look like.

In a similar way, you first imagine who you want to become in your thoughts.

By having a design of who you want to become, you put your RAS to work on finding the strategies and solutions that you need to achieve that design.

> "Everything has been created twice, once on a mental plain and once on a physical plain." - Bob Proctor

Your self-image determines what dreams you permit yourself to pursue.

It determines what choices you allow yourself.
It determines the boundaries which you set.
It determines your attitude and behavior.

It determines the risks you are willing to take.

Without even realizing it, you might have programmed your self-image as a woman who is stressed and overwhelmed. It becomes a self-fulfilling prophecy. Your RAS, which is always hard at work for you, will find evidence and all the reasons why you should be stressed and overwhelmed.

If you think you are a quitter, then your Reticular Activating System will give you evidence of why you need to quit.

If you have the self-image of a woman who never gives up, then you will find all the reasons why you just don't give up.

The surest way to change any behavior is to first change the image that you hold of yourself—only then will you have the eyes to see what is possible beyond your self-limiting beliefs.

I find it fascinating that when the airplane pilot programs the GPS coordinates for the destination, they could hit turbulence and deviate from those coordinates, but no matter what, the plane will land in the coordinates it has programmed. It does not deviate.

How does this relate to your self-image?
You hold in your mind an image of yourself that becomes your GPS. Because your self-image is your GPS, and you won't deviate from the image that you hold of yourself.

So, the great news is that you are not stuck in your current self-image. You have the ability to change the image you hold of yourself through the process of neuroplasticity.

In the Encyclopedia Britannica, neuroplasticity is defined as, "the capacity of neurons and neural networks in the brain to change their connections and behavior in response to new information."

Neuroplasticity is the science that allows you to rewire a new image of yourself.

You can change you.

What you need to do is rewire your thoughts by using repetition to create new neural networks.

In other words, if you are willing to change your self-image and discipline yourself, you can redesign a new version of yourself that fulfills you.

Your self-image is the lid that unlocks your treasure.
It is your GPS to the life you want.

Take some time to think about these questions:

1. What self-image do I want to acquire for myself right now?
2. How do I want to design myself?
3. How would a newly designed positive self-image of me impact the people around me?

Your dreams and the life that you want hinge on the opinion that you hold of yourself.

For you to achieve your dreams, you first need to determine the self-image of a woman who is capable of achieving her dreams.

In order to achieve your wholeness design, you first need to decide on the image of a woman who is whole.

You are responsible for redesigning a whole new version of yourself.

This is my personal script:

"The woman I am now is a result of the woman I designed many moons ago, and the woman I want to become many moons from now is the woman I am intentionally designing right now."

Your Fulfillment is Your Responsibility, and Discipline is the Secret Sauce

What I have outlined for you so far in this book is a Formula for Fulfillment:

To be fulfilled, you need the trifecta: a Dream, a Design, and an action plan to Develop who you need to become.

1. A Dream: You need to have a dream, a vision that helps you aspire to become the woman you were created to be.
2. A Design: Designing a life of wholeness is the infrastructure you need to sustain you, as you pursue dreams that are in harmony with your purpose.
3. Develop: You need to develop the image that you hold of yourself in order to achieve the dream and design the life you want.

The Fulfillment Formula is a blueprint you can use over and over again to take responsibility for your own fulfillment.

Begin by replacing a limiting belief about your self-image by rewiring a new belief.

In the chart below I am going to outline some common limiting beliefs and then offer a replacement script that you can use as a rewire formula (as explained in chapter five).

OLD BELIEF	NEW BELIEF	SCRIPT
"I can't change myself."	The Science of Neuroplasticity gives me evidence that I can change the image that I hold of myself, through the process of repetition.	"At any moment, I can choose the image that I hold of myself."
"It is too hard to change."	Expanding my mindset and acquiring new skills is a lot easier than regret. Life is hard when I lack the skills. If I am willing to *Train-Up*, things that were once hard will become easier.	"Every obstacle can be overcome by acquiring new skills."
"I don't have enough time to invest in me."	If I have time to watch a TV show or scroll through social media for fifteen minutes a day, I have time to invest in myself. Not having time is usually a byproduct of a lack of time management and priority skills. Investing in my ability to grow my skills will be the antidote to not having enough time.	"I am fierce about prioritizing my need to invest in myself because that is what will allow me the freedom to have more time for the things that matter most."

OLD BELIEF	NEW BELIEF	SCRIPT
"I am not disciplined."	Dreaming comes before discipline. Dreaming is the fuel for my discipline. When the dream is crystal clear and I am intentionally bringing my dream to the forefront of my imagination, my dream will become my motivation. The key is to learn how to dream so that the dream stays alive and becomes the fuel to my discipline.	"My dream and the life I am designing are the fuel to my discipline."

Your fulfillment hinges on your ability to personally develop yourself. Personal development is one of the three parts of the Fulfillment Formula. Without it, you will remain an unfulfilled woman.

That is a bitter pill to swallow, but the truth is that life doesn't get better unless we get better.

It was through my husband that I discovered the world of personal development. Soon after I met him, he invited me to his house, and what struck me were the books on his bookshelf.

There were three shelves on that black, beat-up bookshelf, and it was very organized for a bachelor.

The top shelf was full of "How to be the Best Golfer" books. At that time, Ryan taught golf, so he wanted to develop his golfing skills.

His second shelf held titles on "How to Become a Successful Investor." With these, he wanted to develop his wealth mindset.

The third shelf contained personal development books by Tony Robbins, Bryan Tracy, Zig Ziglar, and people I did not recognize at the time. On the corner of that shelf was a tiny little book called, *The ABC's of Choosing a Good Wife*.

I was impressed.
And I am still impressed to this day.

It struck me how intentional and dedicated Ryan was in developing himself.

Before that, I had not personally met a man who was so disciplined. He inspired me to make personal development a part of my life, our marriage, and our family culture.

Today, Ryan leads the charge in mindset training and personal development for our children.

Discipline has become part of the way we have designed our family life. Personal development is about discipline.

Discipline is key to achieving the life you want.
Discipline is how Michael Jordan became the greatest basketball player of all time.
Discipline is how Olympians win gold medals.
Discipline is how you expand your business.
Discipline is my secret weapon to being a mom of eight while building a business.
Discipline is how my marriage continues to grow sweeter after sixteen years.
Discipline brings freedom.

And yet...

Ask a teenager to define the word discipline and you might get a sarcastic laugh. It feels like an obsolete word that used to be part of our history, but now seems to have been replaced with feelings.

Our feelings have become the metric for our decisions. The problem is that our feelings, while valid, can be fickle and not always accurate. Don't get me wrong, we cannot achieve fulfillment without acknowledging how we feel, but we cannot allow our feelings to usurp the need for a disciplined life.

I don't always feel like doing the things that bring out the best in me.
To be honest, I don't feel like nailing myself to this chair right now as I write this book, because I am tired. I would rather sit on the beach and eat fried rice and not work out a day in my life.

Clearly, my feelings, void of reason, could be my demise.

The point I am making here is that we need to be aware of how much we let our feelings guide our decision-making.

Ultimately, our decisions ought to be based on what would bring us closer to our highest good, regardless of how we feel.

But tragically, for many of us, feelings have become the executor of our decisions.

We follow advice such as:

- "Do whatever feels good for you."
- "Whatever you feel like doing (even if it be gossip, binge-watching, or eating), go for it."
- "It's your life, I don't care what you do."

These ideas run rampant in our culture, and are appealing because they are easier than being disciplined.

It does not hold us accountable to our highest good.
It lowers our standard of what we are capable of.
I propose we raise our standards for our own sake.

In our home we use this script, "I do what I don't want to do at the highest level because that's what winners do."

Discipline is following through on our commitments, regardless of whether we feel like doing it or not.

Discipline is about holding ourselves accountable to our commitments.

- I don't always feel like getting up, but I choose to honor my commitment.
- I don't always feel like being nice to my husband, but I choose to discipline my tongue.
- I don't always feel like working on my dreams after I put my kids to bed (because I would rather watch a movie after a long day), but I choose discipline so I can achieve the design for my life.
- I don't feel like cooking a healthy meal or cleaning my house, but discipline pushes me to do the things I do not want to do so that I can have the life I want for my family.
- When I feel like complaining (because it is that time of that month and I feel entitled to being moody), I choose discipline so I don't give myself any excuse to be rude.

There are many reasons why you and I don't feel like being disciplined. There are also a million reasons why discipline is worth the price for the life you want.

Discipline is a word we need to resuscitate back into our culture.

Leaving the dishes to pile up because you don't want to clear them right away makes nighttime cleanup daunting.

Running late is stressful if you don't have a disciplined routine.

Maybe you want to start a business, but the reason you have not is that you lack discipline.

Maybe you are tired of your house being a mess, but the reason why it is in chaos is that you are unwilling to bite the bullet of discipline.

Maybe your kids are overwhelmed because they lack discipline, but the way to teach them discipline is for you to discipline yourself first.

Maybe you want peace of mind, but you are unwilling to discipline your thoughts which will protect your peace. Without being able to manage your mind, life feels like a roller coaster of emotions, full of highs and lows.

Whether you want to write a book, leave a job you hate, make more money, live in peace, or achieve great things in life, you need discipline.

Discipline is the way.

The good that you desire requires you to form your willpower.

Procrastination hurts you.
Snoozing makes you feel unaccomplished.
Overeating does not promote optimal health.
Saying whatever you feel like saying could lead people to not want to be around you. And loneliness hurts.
An undisciplined life is a hard life.

It is hard because you can't taste the fulfillment that is destined for you.

But all you have to do to change that is hold yourself accountable to the commitment you have made.

When a woman understands the significance of a disciplined life, she has no limit to her dreams.

Discipline is the key that unlocks the treasure you want.

The choice is yours! The fulfilling life that you want hinges on your ability to be a disciplined woman.

Here are scripts you can use to rewire your mindset about the importance of a disciplined life. Use the Rewire Formula to help you rewire a more disciplined version of yourself.

- "I am a disciplined woman."
- "I say what I mean and mean what I say."
- "I am disciplined in small and big commitments."
- "I am disciplined with my time."
- "I am disciplined and strategic about how and when I communicate my needs."
- "I am disciplined in my need to gain and grow in new skills."
- "I am disciplined about getting what I want."
- "I am disciplined about saying "no" to myself."
- "I am disciplined with honoring my boundaries."
- "I am disciplined with following through on my commitments."
- "I am a woman of my word."

Discipline is mastery of self.

Discipline is ultimately about *TRAINING-UP*. You must discipline yourself to expand your mindset and skill set, so you can maximize your God-given potential and become who you were created to be.

Train-Up For the Life You Want

Here are a few more questions to ponder. Rate yourself 0-10; "10" means you agree, and "0" means you do not agree. Use these as prompts for your journal.

1. My family of origin modeled, taught, and discussed discipline.
2. I am disciplined in managing my thoughts.
3. I make my decisions based on how I feel.
4. I make my decisions based on my commitments.
5. I am a woman of my word.
6. I follow through on my commitments to myself and others.
7. I know that if I am disciplined, I can achieve my dreams and design for my life.

If you are thinking these ideas are hard because you are far from the life you want, I want you to ask yourself one more question: *Who taught me to discipline myself to create a fulfilling life?*

It is important to acknowledge the pain you have endured if no one showed you how to live a life of discipline.

Your lack of fulfillment may not be your fault, but it does remain your responsibility. You cannot change your past. You cannot continue to dwell, blame, and shame yourself for things you cannot change. It is counterproductive.

Give yourself permission to cry it out, ask for help, journal, and process. Let the pain be your fuel to begin the journey of *Training-Up* for the life you want.

So, how do you *Train-Up*?

You expand your mindset and grow your skill set through a life of discipline.

MINDSET: We define "mindset" as your perception, the lens through which you view the world around you, including yourself. Your goal is to expand your mindset so you can raise your level of awareness. For example, before you started reading this book, maybe you didn't understand the difference between dreams and goals, but now you do, and this awareness can help you identify your dream of the season.

So, if expanding your mindset is your goal, how do you do that?

Read.
Listen to experts, and subscribe to their podcasts.
Study people and learn new ways of seeing the world.

SKILL SET: We define "skill" as the ability to do something well. A skill set is a collection of skills that compound your ability to achieve results.

For example, if you are training to become an Olympic gymnast, then your tumbling skills, jumping skills, dancing skills, and many more compound your ability to perform.

CONSISTENCY: "Consistency" is about building a habit of taking action persistently to achieve what you want.

Exponential Transformation is what you are going for. Exponential meaning that you are not just growing incrementally, but rather, rapidly.

If you live a life of discipline, you will be consistently working to expand your mindset and master new skills in order to turn information into formation. This is your secret to massive transformation.

The Cost of an Underdeveloped Self

The price is high if we are unwilling to personally develop ourselves.

What is the price of an underdeveloped self?

Your life is the ultimate price for ignoring your need to develop yourself.

Process this with me for a moment.

- How do you achieve peace of mind? By disciplining your thoughts.
- How do you create meaningful connections? By developing your conversation skills, listening skills, patience, boundaries, and being trustworthy.
- How do you achieve quality health? By disciplining your body.
- How do you pursue dreams that excite you? By never giving up and learning to rise after failure.
- How do you design a home that is full of joy? By working consistently to develop joy and order.
- How do you develop an intimate relationship that lasts? How do you stay in love, even after years of life together? By investing in yourself so you can inspire your special someone.
- How do you fulfill your purpose? By taking action and developing your patience and persistence at the same time.
- How do you live a life that fulfills who you were created to be? You develop yourself through grit and grace.

The price of an underdeveloped self is that you never fully taste the joy of being fully alive.

The burden of an unfulfilled potential causes restlessness, resentment, and anger.

Our hearts are restless until we grow in harmony with our unique purpose.

When I take my dying breath, I want to hear the words, "Well done, My good and faithful servant!"

I want to go before God knowing I have maximized my full potential and have used it to bring good.

An undisciplined life is a hard life.

But ultimately, it is your choice.

Rules and Freedom

Rules. Who wants rules?
In our current culture, it seems like the idea of giving women rules leads to rebellion.
Most women resist them because it feels like a prison.

Let's break this down for a moment. Instead of thinking about how rules make you "feel," rather, think logically about how a life without rules makes you feel.

Without Rules:

- Driving accidents would be prevalent.
- People could hurt other people and get away with it.
- Anyone can cut in line and create chaos.

You get the point. A country without rules leads to anarchy. Any home or school or company without rules and boundaries would quickly lead to chaos.

In my house with eight kids, there are rules by which we hold each other accountable to protect the harmony, order, and joy in our house. Otherwise, I and everyone in the family would go nuts. If I let my kids do whatever they want to do, our home would be a zoo. Literally, kids flying everywhere.

Rules such as:

- The kitchen is closed at a certain time; you can't eat whenever you want.
- Leave the room cleaner than you found it.
- Saturday morning is a chore day.
- We choose our words and manage our tone and body language.

If I didn't set up the rules, I would be a hot mess and so would my kids.

Rules are not there to suffocate us, but rather to help us interact with each other in a wholesome way.

Rules don't allow us to do whatever we want to do. Rather, they hold us accountable to do what is best for us and the community at large.

I think what we do not like is having rules imposed on us when we do not understand their value. Often, in order to accept the rules, we want to understand what purpose they serve. We want to know the value of the rules and how they affect us.

Rules help us achieve greater freedom. We don't just follow them for the sake of following them. We follow them to protect our freedom.

I want to invite you to a new kind of freedom. A freedom that cannot be taken away from you. It is a freedom that is not dependent on the external circumstances in your life that you cannot control. It is a freedom that allows you to choose the highest version of yourself.

It is a kind of freedom that we deeply crave, it is the kind of freedom that sets our hearts free.

Let me introduce you to 'Interior Freedom.'

In the western world, women have the freedom to vote, own property, choose a career, and choose who they marry.

For the most part, we have what I call exterior freedom, the freedom to choose opportunities.
However, exterior freedom does not equal interior freedom.

So, what is interior freedom?

Interior freedom is having the freedom to choose your highest and best self. Interior freedom is about sustaining a peace of mind that is unshakable.

It allows you to be a pillar amidst the storm of confusion around you.

Interior freedom comes from your ability to choose a response that protects you from external circumstances that are beyond your control.

> "Everything can be taken from a man but one thing: the last of the human freedoms— to choose one's attitude in any given set of circumstances, to choose one's own way."
> –Viktor E. Frankl

Victor Frankl is a holocaust survivor. He explains that our ability to choose how we perceive external circumstances determines the quality of our life.

Today, women have many freedoms, but we are incapable of choosing our highest and best selves because we lack the necessary discipline to make the best choice. Therefore, we are not free.

If you want freedom then you must become disciplined. A lack of discipline makes you susceptible to external circumstances that are beyond your control.

If you are to achieve the peace of mind that you want, then you cannot be a victim of uncontrolled circumstances. What you can control is how you choose to perceive the external circumstances of your life.

You no longer have to be a victim of the ever-changing tides around you.

Interior freedom is your ability to remain peaceful, regardless of what comes your way. Interior freedom is about choosing your attitude and your response.

You can be the victor of your life.

Interior freedom is a universal desire.

This is the part of the book where I invite you to choose your own rules for your interior freedom.

If you want to attain peace of mind, then these rules would be your guideposts to achieving your interior freedom.

You get to choose your own rules. These will not be imposed on you. These are rules you have to impose upon yourself.

If you cannot live a life of discipline and follow through with your own self-imposed rules, then you are not free to choose your highest and best self.

You simply cannot achieve the life you want unless you create interior rules to hold yourself accountable.

So, what you have to keep in mind is to choose a rule that leads you to greater interior freedom; the freedom to choose your highest and best self.

Your self-imposed interior rules are your path to interior freedom.

There is a massive distinction between having freedom and being free. This distinction is the difference between a fulfilled and an unfulfilled woman.

Of course, you can choose a life without interior rules—that is your choice. But understand that there are consequences to a life with no interior rules.

Your life, after all, is your responsibility.

I want to bring awareness to the fact that a life without rules is a dangerous life. I want to walk you out of a false narrative that has been so convoluted that we don't even have language for the pain of having the freedom to do whatever we want.

We are hurting because we believe the lie that 'doing whatever we want' is freedom. It is a bold-faced lie. We need to stop lying to ourselves.

I see a lot of empowering but deceiving quotes that confuse women.

Quotes such as:
"Do whatever you want..."
"Do whatever feels right for you..."
"You do you."

These quotes are deceiving because they are only partially true.

What feels right for you in the moment might not be good for you later. You can't gossip about other women, even if it feels justified, because hurting other people has consequences, both for that person and for you.

Chances are, there will be plenty of drama and division in your life if you follow the mantra of 'doing whatever feels right' for you.

You cannot do whatever you want and be happy.

If that statement were true then I would be able to eat rice and ice cream every day and remain healthy and happy.

But the reality is, it doesn't matter what I think, I am going to pay the consequence for whatever I choose.

There are rules to a beautiful and fulfilling life.

These rules might not be written in stone, but you get to write them in your own heart.

In my opinion, it is a privilege to have the freedom to choose your own interior rules. This is true empowerment; it takes away your shackles. You don't have to live in the prison of a life of "doing whatever you feel like doing," you can free yourself from that prison by learning to choose what is in harmony with your highest good.

This is the ultimate freedom...the freedom to choose who you really want to become.

This is not just about women's empowerment.
This is about equipping you with the tools to fulfill your life purpose.

This is about giving you tools to become who you were created to be for the world!

This is about you "setting the world on fire" by becoming exactly who you were born to be.

So...what kind of rules can you adopt for yourself that will lead to greater interior freedom?

21 Rules For Women

I created a list of twenty one rules where I explain the importance of each rule. Right now, I invite you to process each rule and adopt those that serve you best.

If these rules challenge your beliefs, give yourself permission to wrestle with new ideas that could serve you better in this season of your life.

These self-imposed rules are common sense but not common practice. Read through them and make your own decisions.

The best way to use this list is to first journal the consequences of each rule and then make a decision on your own rules of being a woman. They are not in any particular order. If you want, you can reorder them according to what is important to you.

Remember, interior rules are not regulated by anyone but you alone. You can pick and choose, or not adopt them at all. These are your rules for your life.

The goal is Interior Freedom.

I want to warn you, this section below could be a book in itself. I can only give a quick summary, but take your time to dig deep.

You are responsible for your interior freedom.

1. Rate yourself 0 - 10, "10" means that this rule is something you want to implement because it will have a positive ripple effect on every part of your life. "0" means this rule does not apply to you.
2. Ponder the value of each particular rule by thinking hard about the journal prompt.
3. Consider the REWIRE SCRIPT at the end. Use this to help you rewire a new rule in your life. Reference the Rewire Formula (chapter five) so you can begin the process of replacing limiting beliefs with new beliefs that open doors of possibility for you.

Figure 6.3

21 RULES FOR WOMEN

RULE #1: I choose to honor my unconditional worth. I am unrepeatable and irreplaceable.
RULE #2: I choose a whole version of me that is in harmony with my higher purpose.
RULE #3: I choose to learn from my critics and use my pain as fuel to my resilience.
RULE #4: I choose honesty and integrity. I am fierce about honoring my word.
RULE #5: I choose words that bring hope, not harm.
RULE #6: I choose an attitude of gratitude and generosity. I take responsible for my actions.
RULE #7: I choose to seek the good in all things. I trust that life is happening for me.
RULE #8: I choose to invest in personally developing myself so I can give more of myself.
RULE #9: I choose to go above and beyond. I work hard to develop a life of discipline.
RULE #10: I choose to use my wounds as a compass to my contribution.
RULE #11: I choose to learn from my failures and grow from them.
RULE #12: I choose courage to draw firm boundaries over resentment.
RULE #13: I choose to remain humble, coachable, and challenge my own limiting beliefs.
RULE #14: I choose to take action and focus on solutions that allow me to never give up.
RULE #15: I choose to pursue my dreams as a means to contribute good in the world.
RULE #16: I choose to be patient with progress.
RULE #17: I choose to honor my rest. I respect my rhythm of life.
RULE #18: I choose to cultivate meaningful connections.
RULE #19: I choose to raise my standard by presenting my highest and best self.
RULE #20: I choose wealth as an abundance of time, treasure, and talent for the purpose of generosity.
RULE #21: I choose my thoughts and take responsibility for managing my mind and emotions.

Go to redefinesuccessforwomen.com for a free printable download.

READY?

RULE #1: I choose to honor my unconditional worth, I am unrepeatable and irreplaceable.

Pause for a moment and think about the fact that there will never be another you in this lifetime, neither in the past nor in the future.

Let's break it down. You were born with 100 billion neurons in your brain and a unique set of DNA. All the neurons in your brain were wired in a specific way: your circuitry, your unique connections, and the intricacies woven together, based on your personal experience and aptitude, make who you are entirely unique. All these different variables made you who you are now.

From a scientific level, you can prove to yourself that you are a valuable human being *simply because you're unrepeatable and irreplaceable*. There is no one else who is ever going to be you. No one else will have your DNA tied to your experiences. And not only that, nobody will have all those combinations of who you are in this unique time in history.

You were born in this time of history. All that you experience is unique to this specific time. So there's not only a unique you, who is irreplaceable and unrepeatable, but also circumstantially, the combination of who you are in the context of this time in history can never be replicated.

You need to have a great conviction that who you are is so valuable that you could never be repeated.

In our culture, we consider rarity as something to be of high value, like a diamond. It's so unique and so precious that we put a high price tag on items that are so rare. And yet, if you think about who you are, the dynamic human nature of your unique combination makes you a millionfold more rare than any diamond.

And yet, it doesn't matter what I tell you—it matters how you understand your value. What you need to do is to provide evidence to yourself that you are valuable, therefore what you offer is irreplaceable. What you give to this world, no one else can.

Your value is unconditional. Neither your failures, results, performance, money, fame, nor achievements determine your value. You are valuable simply because you are in this world. You don't need to keep proving yourself. Nothing changes your value. Your value is not for sale.

Journal: What do I think about this interior rule?

REWIRE SCRIPT: "I am unrepeatable and irreplaceable, my worth is unconditional."

RULE #2: I choose a whole version of me that is in harmony with my higher purpose.

Choosing a whole version of you means that you are taking inventory of every part of your arena. You are intentional about how you want every part of your life to be and you are continually working hard to achieve the life that you want. You are paying attention to your needs and you are investing in filling your cup.

A whole version of you means that you have chosen to seek the good in every part of your life, regardless of what the external circumstances might be. You are designing it intentionally with a deep awareness that you cannot control the external circumstances.

Therefore, in order to have interior freedom, you are choosing to see the good in every part of your arena regardless of the circumstances. You are no longer living like a victim. You are choosing to see the good.

This is what I call living from the best-case scenario.
Most of us plan for the worst-case scenario because we are afraid of disappointment. The problem is that we use our Reticular Activating System to find all the worst-case scenarios, which leads us to greater fear and anxiety.

By living in our best-case scenario, we free ourselves from ruminating negative thoughts that encroach on our peace of mind.

This rule helps you to stay firm in honoring the needs of every part of your life. This holds you accountable for staying vigilant in what fulfills you so you can remain whole.

Journal: What do I think about this interior rule?

REWIRE SCRIPT: "I honor my needs in every arena of my life."

RULE #3: I choose to learn from my critics and use my pain to fuel my resilience.

There is no greatness without critics.

Let me bring that down a notch: it doesn't matter if you live under a rock and never do anything to ruffle anyone's feathers, you will have critics.

Critics will never go away.

My own critics have crippled me in the past. They have caused me stress and anxiety, and robbed me of the peace of mind I needed to be present to my family and my work. I have allowed my critics to rob me of my interior freedom; my freedom to choose my highest and best self. The most challenging critics are those who are closest to us; their words somehow sting more. There is just no way around critics.

The reality is, we are human beings who get hurt. It is part of the human condition. We can fight it or we can use it to help us grow in resilience.

Managing critics and using their criticism to grow in resilience is a muscle that gets developed over time. Once you develop it, it gives you strength and courage.

I can pinpoint the pain that critics have inflicted on me to a point where it discouraged me to continue to grow The Woman School. Ryan was so tender with me in moments when I felt shattered by the criticism of people who have no idea what I have gone through. I had no choice but to grow in my resilience skill if I were to continue to serve women.

I have come a long way and I promise you, the sting hurts less, but it doesn't go away completely.

But it can be the very gift you need to develop yourself.

Critics can help you achieve greater resilience—the same resilience you need to pursue your dreams.

If you choose this rule, then you will protect your ability to stay resilient in the face of the harshest criticism. In other words, the sky's the limit to what is possible in your life if you no longer fear your critics.

Journal: What do I think about this interior rule?

REWIRE SCRIPT: "I choose to learn from my critics."

RULE #4: I choose honesty and integrity, I am fierce about honoring my word.

In my house, our children write integrity scripts such as, "I do what is right even when no one is watching." I am fierce about helping my children develop a habit of honesty. It seems like common sense, yet the common practice is dishonesty.

For example, it is all too easy to say,
"I got caught in traffic..." if you are late.
"I did the work..." even if you only did half of it.
"I'm coming..." and if you need to flake, don't worry about it.

Why is dishonesty tolerated?

Why are we living in a culture where we are desensitized by people who lie? We are no longer shocked that our politicians, leaders, and friends lie. We turn the other cheek and we let them get away with deceit.

There is no cultural standard, no moral conduct that holds you accountable to being a woman of your word.

Why is honesty not a rule for us?

Our lies come after us. Either we lie to ourselves, or we lie to other people, and pretend like that is perfectly ok. This is why we hear so much talk about the need for authenticity because it seems to be a rare thing.

Dishonesty creates unnecessary drama because we can't keep track of what is true versus what we have fabricated.

It's like needing a Rolodex for our lies.

When you are dishonest, people eventually find out. Everything in the dark will eventually come to light.

When you lie, people don't trust you. It makes them doubt you. Often, they won't say it to your face, but they know they can't trust you and that you are unreliable.

And then you wonder:

Why don't people like me?
Why won't people help me?
Why are people so rude to me?

To live by a rule in which you hold yourself accountable to be a woman of integrity, where you find the courage, to be honest with yourself and with other people, you set yourself free.

When you choose this rule, you won't have to worry about the lies you fumbled, because you know that you just don't lie.

I had a misunderstanding with my son and he accused me of doing something that I didn't. He was doubting me even though I tried to tell him that it was inaccurate. But before I could give evidence against his false accusations, Ryan quickly jumped in and said, "Your mother doesn't lie, Jack."

I've lied in the past, but I have adopted this rule over the last couple of decades because my mentor drilled its importance into me. I learned the skill of being honest even when no one is watching, even in small and seemingly insignificant things. Thanks to Elena, I discovered that there is no interior freedom without honesty.

I found this rule very helpful in gaining respect from my children, my friends, and my husband.

When we are not honest with ourselves, we are not choosing our highest good.
Deep down, a seed of restlessness begins to sprout.
Honesty and integrity give a woman self-confidence.

The opposite is also true; when a woman lacks integrity and is dishonest, her confidence is a mere facade.

If you adopt this rule, it will simplify your life and draw you one step closer to the interior freedom you crave.

Journal: What do I think about this interior rule?

REWIRE SCRIPT: "I am a woman of integrity."

RULE #5: I choose words that bring hope, not harm.

Having command of the words that come of your mouth is vital to creating meaningful connections. Your words have power. They either bring hope or harm to those around you.

I never really agreed with the adage, "Sticks and stones may break my bones but names will never hurt me."

As you grow in resilience, the words might not hurt as much, however, unless we are numb to our emotions, we are going to feel the pain of hurtful words spoken to us, especially words we speak to ourselves.

What harsh words did you hear growing up?
"You are stupid."
"You are worthless."
"You are never going to amount to anything."

Words have the power to devalue us. They get wired into our thoughts and become a belief that we live by. We quickly reach a point where we don't question them anymore.

Harmful words that we heard growing up can damage our dreams, our hopes, and our ability to make quality decisions.

And the words that we use to criticize ourselves do the most damage because no one can hold us accountable for the negative thoughts that we ruminate.

We inflict pain upon ourselves and use those same harsh words to inflict pain on the people we are called to love.

Words become flesh.

When you spew negativity, it roars back at you.

But when you are intentional about bringing words of hope, life blossoms around you.

You will eventually harvest what you plant. If you are surrounded by negativity, then begin by being mindful of the words that you are allowing yourself to use. Replace words that bring harm with words that bring good.

Compliment people in your thoughts. Don't use words that belittle you. Train your tongue to be a bearer of goodness, not a "Debbie Downer."

I have found that women use harmful words because they lack the skill of communicating words of hope. They just don't have the skill.

They lack the ability to choose positive scripts that would not only serve them but those that they love.

What words do you want to replace in your current vocabulary that can help you become a ray of hope?

Here are some samples phrases. Use them as a guide to help you create and replace illegal words that no longer serve you.

FROM: "This is horrible..."
TO: "It wasn't the best experience, but I can learn from it."
FROM: "It was such a disaster..."
TO: "It was a bit of a dance."
FROM: "I am so stupid..."
TO: "I learn something new every day."
FROM: "I am so overwhelmed..."
TO: "I need to *skill-up*."

When you adopt the rule of using words that bring hope, then you can protect your interior freedom. This rule holds you accountable to a standard of seeking and speaking the good.

Journal: What do I think about this interior rule?

REWIRE SCRIPT: "Words become flesh. I choose words that bring hope, not harm."

RULE #6: I choose an attitude of gratitude and generosity. I take responsibility for my actions.

Attitude is a combination of thoughts, feelings, and behaviors. Attitude determines how you respond to circumstances around you. Attitude impacts the way you make people feel, which then impacts the way people respond to you.

You can control your attitude by controlling your thoughts. Your thoughts influence your feelings and directly impact your actions.

You can take responsibility for your actions by choosing thoughts of gratitude and generosity.

Make no mistake, people around you experience your attitude, either good or bad. You can't fake it forever, and you can't fake it all the time.

My children understand that their attitude either opens or shuts doors for them. Their attitude is a choice with consequences.

A crapitude (meaning crappy attitude) will quickly determine what they will be allowed to do or not do. I want them to understand that their attitude is the determining factor in achieving what they want.

I am not advocating manipulation, that would be insincere and lead to unfulfillment. What I am saying is that you can create a habit of gratitude and generosity that is sincere. And when you do, doors of opportunities open.

> "You can't be grateful and angry at the same time." –Tony Robbins

An ungrateful woman complains about what she does not have instead of focusing on what she does have.

By choosing an attitude of gratitude, you can find grace in challenging moments and use it as means of generosity.

Rule #6 protects your interior freedom because it gives you control over your actions as opposed to finding something or someone to blame for your frustrations. You get to choose how you respond to the external circumstances that come your way and that is the ultimate freedom.

Journal: What do I think about this interior rule?

REWIRE SCRIPT: "I am a woman of gratitude and generosity."

RULE #7: I choose to seek the good in all things, I trust that life is happening for me.

It is easy to complain about why life is not happening the way I want it. I find this to be especially true in building a business.
I always say that teaching is my passion, business has become my path to discipline and my critics have become my source of strength.

My company has helped to chisel me in more ways than I wanted. I never imagined myself going into business, so I never prepared for it. I just jumped in head first because I was passionate about helping women. What this meant was, I made a lot of mistakes. I hired people who took advantage of me or directly betrayed me. There were hard moments.

But what I learned is that choosing to see that life is happening for me helped me see opportunities amid heartaches and frustrations.

Ryan and I have a script, "This is happening for us, babe." Amazingly, things always worked out for the better, but I know this is because I was putting my RAS to work to find the good in those not-so-grand situations.

I heard my daughter say, "I was really upset that I didn't get chosen for the role I wanted in our school play, but I know it was life happening for me, mom."

Seeing how much my children have been impacted by these rules gives me so much hope. If we can equip our future generation sooner, then they can avoid the unnecessary suffering that distracts them from pursuing their purpose.

Every challenge comes with opportunity, we just need the eyes to look for it.

If you adopt this rule, you can turn every challenge into a gift. You can protect your interior freedom when you choose the core belief that life is always happening for you.

This will give you greater peace of mind if you trust that good can come even from our brokenness.

Journal: What do I think about this interior rule?

REWIRE SCRIPT: "Life is happening for me and not to me."

RULE #8: I choose to invest in personally developing myself so I can give more of myself.

When you do good, the hormone oxytocin is released into your body, which makes you feel good about yourself. It is the law of giving and receiving: the more you give, the more you receive the joy that comes from giving.

Imagine designing a life in which you are very intentional about creating opportunities to genuinely serve people around you, without expecting anything in return.
For true generosity to occur, we have to be detached from the outcome.

That is not easy.

Giving freely without the expectation of anything in return protects us from false expectations. Some people are simply incapable of giving back, so by letting go of what we get in return, we free ourselves from resentment.

It certainly makes us feel better when someone is grateful for our generosity, but our peace of mind cannot be dependent on how people respond. That is a volatile gauge.

It is important to note that you could be trapped in a mindset where you are giving as a way to seek validation.

Generosity will always come back to you. The giver always receives. It might not be from the person you are giving to, but you will be rewarded for the good that you do.

However, it is vital to point out that it will be very challenging to keep giving unless you are consistently receiving the nourishment that you need to fill your cup.
When you are running on empty, it is harder to give without expecting anything in return. You are less patient.

The prerequisite to sustainable generosity is receptivity.

Investing in yourself is an investment in the people you love. The same is true when you do not invest in yourself—you rob the people you love.

If you adopt this rule, it will help you stay vigilant against the burnout that causes anxiety and stress, and holds you back from choosing your highest and best self.

Journal: What do I think about this interior rule?

REWIRE SCRIPT: "Investing in myself is investing in the people I love, therefore it is my duty."

RULE #9: I choose to go above and beyond. I work hard to develop a life of discipline.

"I can't stand cheap work."

This is the script I use for my children when I am frustrated about a task done with only the bare minimum effort.

I ask them, "Do you see yourself as someone who does the bare minimum? Or do you go above and beyond?"
They don't usually answer, but I know that I am planting a seed that I hope will hold them accountable for doing great work someday.

To do any great work, you have to go above and beyond.

As a business owner, I am hyper-vigilant of employees who only do the bare minimum. It is toxic to the company.

The mentality of, "What is the least I can do?" makes us feel insecure around women who go above and beyond.

Yet when you are confident about your work ethic, it contributes to your self-confidence.

People who have a disciplined work ethic, and go above and beyond, automatically create opportunities for themselves.

Doors open for people who go the extra mile.

Who doesn't want to hire or help someone who has an "above-and-beyond" work ethic?

On the contrary, doors shut if we are undisciplined and do only the bare minimum.

I am constantly trying to raise my children's standards. And it is definitely a work in progress.

By choosing to make this rule a part of your life, you give yourself a better chance for the doors of opportunity to open for you.

Journal: What do I think about this interior rule?

REWIRE SCRIPT: "How I do anything is how I do everything. I go above and beyond."

RULE #10: I choose to use my wounds as a compass for my contribution.

No one lives pain-free. It is an inevitable part of the human experience. Some of the greatest pain we endure can also become a great source of wisdom.

We don't always see the wisdom behind our wounds, but if we search for it, it will eventually find us. Using our wounds as a compass towards our contribution helps us to focus not on our gap but on our gain. We get to choose our lens.

My own suffering has been my fuel in building The Woman School. My passion for serving women came from years of tears.

When I look back at my life, I can celebrate the trials and heartaches, and see the good that they have brought about. It doesn't take away the pain or the injustice, it just helps me channel my focus.

Adopting this rule allows you to remain hopeful in challenging moments.

Journal: What do I think about this interior rule?

REWIRE SCRIPT: "My wounds are my compass to my contribution."

RULE #11: I choose to learn from my failures and grow from them.

In my house we have a GFG dinner tradition: we go around the table and each person talks about Gratitude, Failure, and Growth (GFG). Each person shares something they are grateful for, one way they failed, and what they learned from that failure (how they grew).

Ryan and I are adamant about teaching our children to be grateful for their failures as a means of growth.

Fear of failure often stems from a fear of being unlovable. We each have an innate need to be loved. So, if we are in an environment where we feel more lovable if we achieve perfection, or are scorned for our failures, we develop an understanding that love is conditional. We start to believe in the lie that we must prove our worth.

Young minds cannot create distinctions.

It is natural to assume that failure makes us unlovable. Inevitably, we develop a fear of failure because we are afraid of not being worthy of love.

Most of the time our parents are unaware that they are promoting fear when they put conditions on our lovability. Nonetheless, it happens: if the love you receive is conditional, you will feel like you have to prove yourself worthy of love.

If I told you that *failure is part of growth* and that no great person who walked the face of the earth did everything perfectly, would that be enough to convince you to not be afraid of failure?

Your answer will give you insight regarding your fear of failure or your freedom to fail.

If you have been conditioned to be afraid of failure, then you will need to shift your belief to see the value that failure brings to your life.

To attain interior freedom, you must be free to fail and grow from it.

Journal: What do I think about this interior rule?

REWIRE SCRIPT: "I fail forward fast and learn from it."

RULE #12: I choose courage to draw firm boundaries over resentment.

I first heard the phrase, "Courage over resentment," from Brené Brown. Honestly, it was a massive shift in my mind: I finally realized how much division and drama I suffered from my lack of courage to draw firm boundaries.

I fell into a pattern of harboring resentment because I assumed that people should already know the boundaries I needed.

I assumed others could read my mind...silly me.
I was wrong and I suffered for it.

I did not know how to draw firm boundaries. I was afraid of losing the other person, so I chose instead to lose myself.

When we lack the courage to communicate our boundaries effectively, we create division. A lack of boundaries creates monsters around us and within us.

A seed of resentment grows within us when we allow our boundaries to be crossed because we have not communicated them firmly. Anger begins to build.

If we can't communicate our boundaries, others grow entitled to their ill behavior. And the next thing we know, there is a massive fight. It is our responsibility to draw that line. I learned this the hard way, and many times over.

Now, every time I feel that my boundaries are crossed, I find the courage to create the necessary boundary before the monsters of resentment turn into monsters of rage.

We cannot grow in interior freedom if we are growing seeds of anger and resentment. We have to learn how to communicate our needs efficiently and effectively.

Regardless of how people respond to the boundaries you set, you have done your part to protect your interior freedom. You can only control yourself.

Journal: What do I think about this interior rule?

REWIRE SCRIPT: "I choose courage over resentment."

RULE #13: I choose to remain humble and coachable, and challenge my own limiting beliefs.

The most challenging women to coach are those who feel like they know it all.

In reality, they are not coachable. They get defensive and blame everyone else.

I can't introduce a new idea, because they find something wrong with it.
I can't hold them accountable, because they make excuses.
I can't give them constructive feedback, because they don't take it well.

You can't teach someone who knows it all.

Maybe this uncoachable woman is you. And if it is, you can change this habit. That is the best part.

The most accomplished people in the world have coaches.

Why? Because people who have accomplished great things see the value in coaching.

Unless you are coachable, you will remain stuck year after year. Unless you are open to being challenged, own up to your mistakes, and receive feedback with humility, you could be suffering from a limiting belief that is hindering you from going to the next level.

Humility is the foundation of being coachable. A humble heart will give you wings to fly.

This rule will allow you to grow and become who you were created to be. Without it, you will feel stifled and unfulfilled. Unfulfillment leads to restlessness and encroaches on our peace of mind. Your interior freedom can only be attained and sustained when your heart is fulfilled.

Journal: What do I think about this interior rule?

REWIRE SCRIPT: "I am humble and coachable."

RULE #14: I choose to take action and focus on solutions that allow me to never give up.

Diana kept waiting for the right moment to find another job. She felt anxious all the time and hated her current job, it drained her. She kept going back and forth, afraid of making the wrong choice. She kept comparing herself to her friends who loved their jobs and seemed to be happy. She didn't connect the dots that her anxiety came from her indecision, which made her feel insecure. Three years later, she is still in the job she hates, but now she hates herself. She finds herself saying things like, "I did everything I could. It never worked. I tried so hard. I'm done trying."

When we don't take action and find solutions, eventually, we give up on our own life. We will settle into a life that we don't want because we are paralyzed by indecision, and stuck in inaction.
In The Woman School we say, "Even God can't steer a parked car."

My dad would always say to me, "If there is a will, there is a way."

If we don't give up, we will eventually find our way up. It might not look like what we originally envisioned, but if we keep trying, our reality will supersede our vision.

Taking action is half the battle. If you train yourself to take the first action step then the next step will reveal itself.

The Woman School started as a dream. I did not have all the answers on how to build an online school. I decided to create a masterclass before I even thought of creating an infrastructure. Still, every action revealed the next set of options for me.
Even when I did not make the best decisions, they still lead me one step closer to the dream.

Being a woman of action means you don't have to be stuck in a life you don't want. You are capable of taking the next step and finding solutions that expand possibilities.

There is no way to find out unless you take that next brave step forward.

The rule of taking action and never giving up allows you to grow into an elevated version of yourself. As you grow, so does your ability to choose your highest and best self.

Journal: What do I think about this interior rule?

REWIRE SCRIPT: "I am a woman of action and solution."

RULE #15: I choose to pursue my dreams as a means to contribute good in the world.

Can you summarize your dream of the season right now?
How would fulfilling this dream contribute good to the people around you?

If your answer is, "I don't know what my dream of the season is..." that is okay. You are not alone.

Most women don't realize that every season of life has a unique dream ready to be birthed. But, it requires labor.

You first need to discover the dream, then labor toward giving birth to that dream. To dream is to have a vision that inspires hope in you.

A woman without a vision perishes because, without a destination, it is easy to wander aimlessly. You will feel a lack of purpose because there is no clarity in where you want to go or who you want to become. Life will feel dull.

Your dream is like a compass to your contribution in this unique season of your life. My contribution in this current season of my life has everything to do with me giving birth to this book. It is what I am called to pursue right now. Writing this book gives me life because it fulfills my call at this moment in time.

The ultimate purpose of your dreams is to bring greater purpose to those around you. Why? Because living your purpose inspires those around you to live their purpose.

What a great contribution to know that you are inspiring someone else to fulfill their unique purpose of the season.

If your dream is unclear, you will feel a sense of restlessness. That restlessness is evidence that parts of you are waiting to be fulfilled.

This rule of pursuing your dreams allows you to feel alive.

Journal: What do I think about this interior rule?

REWIRE SCRIPT: "I am a woman of vision and purpose."

RULE #16: I choose to be patient with progress.

I can be very impatient when it comes to pursuing my dreams, but my impatience causes me unnecessary suffering.

I had to be very patient to find a man like Ryan. I had to work for five years before I made money in business. I had to plan for two years before I could move to our dream home in Florida.

I try to laugh at my impatience, but it feels like a war inside of me.

It is so easy for me to bypass the progress and focus on why I am not there yet. I have to constantly script myself into patience. My script is, "I have to go slow to go fast."

To protect your interior freedom, you have to be patient with your progress and honor the journey.

With a lot of patience, you can achieve great things in life.

Journal: What do I think about this interior rule?

REWIRE SCRIPT: "I am patient with my progress."

RULE #17: I choose to honor my rest. I respect my rhythm of life.

When your body isn't working well, nothing is working well.

Your body is the vehicle through which you can accomplish your divine purpose. You have to learn to be a good steward of your body so you can go the distance and maximize your full potential.

In a very busy world where we are pulled in every direction, it takes firm boundaries to create a rhythm of life that honors the body's need for nourishment and rest.

Your body is a sacred vehicle in which you can fulfill your unique purpose. Therefore, you must be intentional about taking care of it.

Keeping this rule will help you treat your body with greater reverence and not squander your energy on meaningless things. You have to pay attention to what your body is telling you. You have to make sure that you give it enough nourishment so that it can function at an optimal level.

When you are exhausted, you are vulnerable to frustration. Any little thing could set you off and rob you of your interior freedom.

But when you create a rhythm of life that honors your need for rest, you give yourself the best chance to fulfill your dreams and your wholeness design.

Journal: What do I think about this interior rule?

REWIRE SCRIPT: "I honor my rhythm of life and respect my body's need for rest."

RULE #18: I choose to cultivate meaningful connections.

The relationships we choose to cultivate determine the quality of our life. When our relationships drain us, we feel lonely and depleted. When our relationships nourish the depths of our souls, we feel satisfied and inspired.

We are made for connection. Our hearts long to love and be loved. When we prioritize cultivating meaningful connections, it impacts how we show up to the souls around us. It doesn't matter how much money we have if our hearts are void of deep connections. Money cannot cure our loneliness.

The rule of cultivating meaningful connections and prioritizing your need to bring value to the people you love most is crucial. There is so much joy that comes from deep and meaningful connections.

You have a choice to surround yourself with superficial conversations that leave you empty or find people who will nourish the deepest parts of you.

You get to decide who you want around you to influence you.

When you prioritize your human need for connection, then you stand a greater chance at protecting your interior freedom.

Journal: What do I think about this interior rule?

REWIRE SCRIPT: "I choose relationships that respect and honor my value."

RULE #19: I choose to raise my standard by presenting my highest and best self.

In my house, I tell my children that how they present themselves is a form of contribution. "When you smell bad, you rob people of quality air." This is my attempt to bring humor into what can be a very challenging concept for teenagers.

In my opinion, we have downgraded our standards of how to show up. It is not just about the clothes we wear or our hygiene habits (although that is foundational), but it is also our politeness and our ability to take responsibility for how our presence can impact the people around us.

The way we show up has a ripple effect.

If you smile at the clerk who had a bad morning with her daughter, maybe it eases her heart enough to inspire her to apologize to her daughter, which could improve their relationship.

You would never know the extent of the impact of your smile.

These micro-moments, though seemingly insignificant, can have macro significance in someone's life. Living your little moments well by presenting your highest and best could be the difference that someone needed to rise from their ashes.

When you get ready in the morning, ask yourself, "How can I show up and present my best self today so I can inspire someone?"
How you dress, talk, and walk, and your facial expressions can all be used as an opportunity to bring joy.

Contribution doesn't have to be grand, it can be done so beautifully in little ways.

Nothing is wasted if we find the opportunity to serve at every given moment, be it the way we brush our hair, our smile, our body language, or our politeness. All of these can change the culture of a room from negative to positive.

You walk into so many rooms in your lifetime—be intentional about showing up as your highest and best self.

If you are strategic and intentional about making your very presence an act of generosity, then you can do so much good by making the ordinary, extraordinary.

Your goal is to learn the skill of making people feel important by how you show up.

The rule of showing up as your highest and best self will give you peace in knowing that you have done your part to make the ordinary extraordinary, and that is fulfilling.

Journal: What do I think about this interior rule?

REWIRE SCRIPT: "I present my highest and best self."

RULE #20: I choose wealth as an abundance of time, treasure, and talent for the purpose of generosity.

Wealth is not just about money, it is so much more than that. You can have a lot of money and still feel worthless. True wealth is about having an abundance mindset.

Abundance, as we define it, is living in a perpetual state of gratitude and generosity.

A woman who lives with a grateful heart has a greater capacity to give back because she sees everything as a gift.

When you hold yourself accountable for using your time wisely, you feel at peace with yourself. There is no guilt because you are giving all you've got.

When you cultivate your talent there is a sense of satisfaction in knowing that you are maximizing your full potential.

When you use your treasure (money and other resources) as a way to serve people around you, you feel good about who you are.

True wealth ought to give you a sense of peace that what you offer the world is beyond the material goods, it is an abundance mindset.

Having an abundance mindset is living with a profound trust that there is always more than enough to go around.
It is having faith that your time, treasure, and talent are being used for a greater cause.

Journal: What do I think about this interior rule?

REWIRE SCRIPT: "I am a wealthy woman."

RULE #21: I choose my thoughts and take responsibility for managing my mind and emotions.

The first time I heard that I had the ability to manage my thoughts and not allow myself to think about whatever comes into my mind, it literally blew my mind.

The idea that I had control over my thoughts shattered so many other limiting beliefs that were holding my dreams back.

The idea of training my mind by controlling what I focused on gave me the path to sustained peace of mind. If I'd had this training sooner, it could have saved me from so much unnecessary stress and anxiety.

Ruminating on negative thoughts is dangerous. We release stress hormones by simply revisiting the same thoughts over and over again.

Furthermore, when we don't manage our thoughts, we develop a habitual pattern of ruminating on negative thoughts, inducing the cortisol hormone and creating a negative, compounding impact on our bodies. There is plenty of evidence that demonstrates that thoughts alone can make us sick. Negative thoughts create unnecessary stress on our bodies. It is not healthy.

Think of someone who betrayed you many months or years ago. When you remember what they said to you, do you start to feel anxious, even though it took place so long ago?

Our thoughts impact our emotions. The reason why so many women suffer through emotional roller coasters is that we have not been trained to manage our thoughts and our thoughts can influence our emotions.

So many women are suffering from the burden of ruminating negative thoughts. They suffer because they bleed those negative thoughts into every part of their arena and the next thing they know, life is just "horrible."

And to make it worse, everyone around us feels that negativity and they also suffer for it.

Adopting the rule of managing your thoughts is not just an investment in your interior freedom, but it is also an investment in the people you love.

An anxious mother can create anxious children. An overwhelmed woman is not pleasant to work with. A stressed woman has a hard time with deep intimacy because it is hard to be fully present in the moment.

Your ability to manage your thoughts is key to your interior freedom. When you stay vigilant against negative thoughts, you give yourself the gift of sustained peace.

Journal: What do I think about this interior rule?

REWIRE SCRIPT: "I am fierce in managing my mind and my emotions."

Now, you get to decide: which rule(s) do you want to adopt for your interior freedom? Why? Are there others you would add? Feel free to write your own personal rules.

Consider which rules could protect your peace.

These rules are yours to choose.

Use the scripts to rewire your mindset and allow them to become the fuel for your life of discipline.

When you decide to personally develop yourself, you get to choose the rules that help you achieve success that is rooted in fulfillment.

These are not imposed upon you. You are imposing them on yourself.

The goal is to taste the true freedom that comes from within. You don't have to be a victim of the external circumstances in your life. You can make the good, and the not-so-good, become great in your eyes.

These are your rules.
This is your choice.
This is your life.
It is the only one you have.
The more you invest in yourself, the greater your results will be.

Having freedom is not the same as being free. Freedom is your birthright. Interior freedom is your right to be fully alive.

Pause
Ponder
Act

Chapter 6

1. What has a lack of discipline cost you?
2. How would your life change if you adopted the *21 Rules of Being a Woman*?
3. What rule would you create for yourself?

CHAPTER 7

SUCCESS IS YOUR CHOICE

1. Nothing Changes Your Value
2. Our Differences Should Not Divide Us
3. Where Do You Go From Here?
4. Redefine Success For You
5. My Hope For You

Nothing Changes Your Value

I can see Miss Rosa's beautiful smile, it still comforts me when I think of her.

She was the janitor at my children's school.
She cleaned the tables meticulously with a huge smile on her face. The children loved her.

She barely spoke English but it didn't matter because her warm presence communicated so much more.

There was a sincerity and humility about her.

I get teary-eyed thinking about her and the love she planted in those children's hearts. I have not seen her in almost a decade and yet, she has impacted the way I want to treat people. I don't think she realizes how much of an impact she had on me. I am truly grateful for who she is.

I wonder if she feels successful. I wonder if she considered herself small or insignificant. It makes me sad to think that she would probably never consider herself worthy of a successful life. She could not boast of glamor or fame. She had no fortune or prestige.

She carried none of our culture's markers of success, yet, she had left an indelible mark on my soul.

How can we allow someone like Miss Rosa, who had such a significant impact on my life, to feel insignificant?

How many more women feel unsuccessful because, in their minds, they have failed to achieve the metric of success that our culture has instilled in us?

If we want true empowerment, then we CANNOT allow women to feel that their worth is conditional on what they can offer the world. Women should feel successful when they fill other people's cups.

We need a new movement.

- A movement that gives all women a blueprint for fulfillment.
- A movement that focuses on our deep desire to be fulfilled while in pursuit of the things we love.
- A movement that honors our irreplaceable value in the world.
- A movement that values all women.
- A movement where ALL women understand from a very deep level that their value NEVER changes.

Nothing changes your value.
You are valuable simply because you exist.

Your failures or your success do not make you more or less valuable.
What you produce does not define your value.
Your performance does not define your value.

You don't need to keep proving that you are valuable enough.

You are valuable regardless of what you achieve or do not achieve.
You are valuable regardless of whether people value or devalue you; their opinions do not change your value.

We need a movement that honors the value of every human being.

We need every woman to HONOR her own value.
We need every woman to OWN her unconditional worth.
We need every woman to know that her life MATTERS.
We need every woman to know that what she offers the world, NO ONE CAN.
We need every woman to take responsibility for the gift of her life.
We need every woman to take a stand and fight for her value.
We need every woman to honor other women's values.
We need a new army of women who will lead the charge in fighting for women's worth.
We need an army of women who can stay united regardless of their differences.
We need warriors who will lead with empathy and humility.
We need fierce warriors who will stop the vicious cycle of division that is blinding us from the wisdom that we can gain from each other.

We need women to value each other.

To stop the judgment.
To stop the comparison.

To stop valuing people based on what they can or can't offer the world.

No woman should have to suffer the pain of self-doubt.
No woman should have to prove to everyone else that her life is worthy of honor and significance.

No life is insignificant.

Your life is no less important than Oprah's, Mother Teresa's, or Miss Rosa's.

Do you hold the same reverence for Oprah, Mother Teresa, yourself, or Miss Rosa? Who is more important in your eyes?

We should learn to treat every woman with the dignity and respect that they deserve, no matter what they accomplish, great or small.

Is it unfair to have to earn the right to be respected?
We deserve respect.
We deserve to respect ourselves.

We need to stop judging women based only on their appearance, accomplishments, and accolades. We need to get rid of these exterior metrics of what makes a woman more or less valuable.

We have to be part of the solution.

Right now, you have a metric by which you qualify women's value.

How do you know?

If I told you that Oprah was going to visit your house in the next hour, would you frantically clean your house in the same way if you knew that Miss Rosa would pay you a visit in an hour?

If you answer that you would clean your house equally for both women then you are a gem, but it is not the common response.

This is a simple exercise that we can use to hold ourselves accountable for how we treat every woman. Do we truly believe in equality, meaning every woman is equal in value?

We each need to examine our own conscience and do our part to fight the war against our worth.

Our goal ought to be that we see every human being as valuable. Period.

Every human being is valuable regardless of their accomplishments or lack thereof.

Can you imagine how free you would feel when you can celebrate women around you, without putting them into boxes, according to your own judgments?

You can look at an IG post of a beautiful woman, with a nice home and a loving marriage and say to yourself, "Wow, I wonder how much discipline she had to endure in order to achieve that beautiful life she now has? I want to learn from her."

What a shift of perspective!

You don't have to be the judge of how "fake" or "true" her posts are, this is irrelevant. When you judge her, you rob her. When you judge her, you rob yourself.

Make no mistake that the judgment you cast on her is the same metric you are using for yourself! When you devalue another woman, you use that same metric to devalue yourself.

That same metric of judgment that you are using to make women feel small is the same metric you are using to make yourself feel small.

Often, we judge others because we don't believe we are good enough.

The problem is, when we see someone who we think *is* better than us, we feel small.

This is why a woman who gives up a high-paying job feels shame—she believes that she gave up her value (which was tied to her high-paying job) in exchange for time with her children. So now, she is ashamed for being "less valuable." Money was the reason she felt valuable, so when money was gone, so too was her value.

Why should a stay-at-home mom feel less valuable than a corporate mom?
Why should a 100 million dollar CEO feel more important than her housekeeper?
Why should her housekeeper feel that her life is less important than her boss's?

Why should our choice to work or not work determine our value?
Why should a Gucci bag make us feel significant and a bag from Walmart embarrass us?
Why does it matter what we have or don't have if the things that we have do not change our value? Unless, of course, we think it does.

Money does not make us more or less valuable unless we allow money to determine our value.

If we are going to truly empower women, we first have to train women to understand that their value never changes.

Your value never changes.

When you understand from a very subconscious level that you are valuable then you are free to make the best decisions for your life.

Your decision to work or not work does not change your value so you are free to make the best decisions for you and your family. You don't have to be ashamed of your choice.

You don't have to be worried about becoming less important as a result of the difficult choices you have to make.

In the same way, you don't need to make other people feel small because you have achieved more than them.

Your choices matter, but they do not under any circumstance change your value.

When we know that our failures do not make us a failure then we are free to take risks and explore what is possible for us.

So much of the division between women is caused by our own insecurity. There is too much drama when we judge what makes women less or more important than us. We complicate our relationships.

But, we can make them less complicated.
We can change the foundation of our belief that *every human being is valuable.*

Every woman is valuable.

Period.

No conditions necessary.

One of my first homework assignments from my mentor Elena was to get rid of comparison and competition.

When I came to her, I was aching from loneliness.
I had pulled away from my circle of friends because I felt empty. Our conversations were shallow and I was tired of wasting my time on conversations that I felt were void of depth. I wanted meaningful friendships.

For a whole year, I felt so alone.
I cried tears of loneliness.
I would look at other women and wish I was them because I felt that they were better than me.
I wished I was better than me.

Being insecure is painful. It's like seeing something you want and knowing you are not deserving of it. My pain caused me to judge other women. I was jealous and wanted what they had.

Elena knew right away that I was in pain because I was steeped in comparison and competition, though I didn't know it at that time. So for three months she helped me work through my insecurities by the completing the following:

1. Write a list of women who made me feel insecure.
2. Write a list of what I admired about them.
3. Emulate what I admired about them.
4. Compliment them in my head each time I thought about them.

I was a student, so I did exactly as she told me. I realized that the things I felt insecure about were things I could change. I could learn.

When I learned to emulate the good that I saw in them, I was no longer stuck wishing I was them—I could be just like them. That changed the way I looked at women; instead of seeing another woman as my competitor, she became my role model. It felt like a lid was blown off and I started to see other women as a source of wisdom. Every woman was now my ally, not my foe.

The more I saw a woman's value, the more I saw my own value.
The more I acknowledged my value, the more I was able to acknowledge other women's values.

Elena rewired my brain from comparing and competing with others, to celebrating them! I learned to celebrate people simply because they were alive. I had so much more to learn, but that skill gave me interior freedom.

We can never stop learning because learning is not about an arrival, but rather an evolution to our higher self.

Elena taught me to see people with a pure heart.

I still wrestle with judgment every now and then, but I also know that when I do, I am only hurting myself. I can now hold myself accountable because she wired my brain to see the value of every human being.

I cannot put into words what that simple homework did for my peace of mind.
The training that she put me through is the same training I use to free women from the bondage of comparison.

Yes, you can absolutely rewire your brain out of the unhealthy habit of judging and comparing yourself.

You can free yourself from the prison of unhealthy competition. You can design your self-image to be a woman who celebrates other women.

Imagine the light you bring to a room when you understand the value of every woman.

Perhaps you won't have to be so worried about what people think of you.

You don't have to ruminate on your failures—maybe you can laugh at yourself and not take yourself too seriously when you make a mistake.

Perhaps, you will dare greatly. Perhaps, you won't be afraid to chase that big dream that you've been afraid of because you were afraid of what people might think if you fail.

That homework truly changed the way I valued women, but more importantly, it changed the way I valued myself.

I realized how much I devalued myself in the past.
I realized that I, too, was a victim of a false metric of success.

I needed to fight for my own value before I recognized other women's value.

I am not less valuable when I am sixty pounds overweight after having a baby.

My value does not change because of my weight.

I am not less or more valuable for having eight children.
My children do not raise or lower my value, I am valuable simply because I am.

I am not less or more valuable because of my status or age.
I am valuable regardless of my size, skin, or age.

I am not less valuable for shopping at Walmart.
My value does not change because of the Chanel glasses that Ryan gave me.
Wearing Gucci does not make me more valuable than carrying my dollar-store tote.

I don't need to buy brand-name clothes to make me feel more valuable. I can buy fancy or cheap clothes because I like them, not because it makes other people like me.

I was not less valuable when I was not making money. My value has not changed now that I have built a multimillion-dollar company.

My money does not make me more or less valuable. I am valuable regardless of what I earn or do not earn.

I was not less valuable when I received C's on my college paper because of grammar. I am not more valuable now that I am an author.

Your opinion of this book won't change my value—it might hurt me or make me feel good, but it won't change my value.

I was not less valuable when I was in a relationship where I felt devalued. I am valuable regardless of how a man sees my value.
I am valuable apart from my relationship with Ryan.
His love for me does not make me less or more valuable as a woman.

I was not less valuable living in a tiny studio apartment full of thrift store furniture. I am not more valuable now that I can afford velvet couches.
My house, shack, or mansion does not determine my value.

Your opinion of me does not change my value.
Not even my opinion of myself changes my value.

Nothing changes your value.
Just as nothing changes my value.

Every woman is valuable, but not everyone knows their value.

We have to empower women to fight for their value first.

You cannot fight for women's values unless you value yourself.

There is such a need for us to neurologically rewire our bad habits of judgment, comparison, and unhealthy competition. We have to rewire new habits of complimenting and celebrating women, regardless of our differences.

Let's start this movement. Let's have these hard conversations. It is time for us to fight this battle together. Our differences should not divide us.

Our Differences Should Not Divide Us

Billions of women have lived on this earth, and not one woman was the same. Our DNA is proof of our uniqueness. If that is not enough proof for you, then think of the intricate combination of your experiences, circumstances, and time in history. The probability that someone shares your intricate combination is a zillion percent unlikely.

You are simply rare.

We are all uniquely different.

Our intricate combination shapes the way we view the world. Our perception of the world shapes our opinion. We are all on a unique journey together, each on our own path, doing the best with what we know.

The fact that we are so uniquely different is what makes us so beautiful.

Can you imagine if we were all the same?
The dynamism of the human person is so fascinating to witness. We should all be fascinated by each other.

Why do our differences, cause division?
Why do we automatically judge people who do not share our vantage point?

Why are we afraid of people who are different from us?
Why do we assume that people who have different beliefs are a threat to us?

We share a lot in common as human beings. There is good in every person. Even the worst of criminals have some spark of goodness in them. Even our worst enemies can teach us something good. Is it possible for us to laugh and share a meal with someone with opposing beliefs?

Can you see yourself genuinely curious about how someone came to the conclusion about what they believe?

Can you imagine that level of empathy, humility, and kindness?

Why do we automatically judge women who think differently from us?

Why?

If we could lower our guard and our pride, then maybe we could see that every person is not free from pain and that they too have endured the suffering that has contributed to their beliefs. Maybe, we need to start seeing people in their stories and not just their opinions. Maybe, we need to learn to see people with eyes of wholeness.

How can we begin to create world peace when we cannot even have peaceful conversations?

Can you see yourself being open to learning from a woman who does not share your religious, political, or social beliefs? Can you imagine living in a culture where you can be firm in your beliefs while also being tender to those who do not share what you believe?

We have to stop living in camps where we cast judgments on people we don't fully understand.

How much more peaceful can we be if we learn to be united even in our differences?

Maybe, we could actually attain peace in our world, a peace that comes from within.

Where Do You Go From Here?

Where do you go from here?

What do you do when you are finished with this book?

This book should be the beginning of your growth journey.

I hope that you give yourself time to allow the concepts that I am teaching you to penetrate your everyday life.

As Jim Rohn said, "Nothing will change unless you change."

When you get better, you will see everything else get better.

You can begin by making a decision to invest in your fulfillment and achieve the life you want. The first step is to take action.

Here are your concrete action steps:

STEP 1: Go to thewomanschool.com and take the Wholeness Quiz and find out what part of your arena is most vulnerable. Identify how it impacts every part of your life.

STEP 2: Find a mentor who is equipped in giving you the mindset and skill set training you need in order to design a life of wholeness. You cannot do this on your own. (Olympic gold medalists wouldn't be Olympic gold medalists without a coach!) When you invest in a coach, they hold you accountable for achieving your goals faster. Investing in a mentor will save you time and money in the long run.

STEP 3: Read or listen to personal development books daily to help you expand your mind.

STEP 4: Create a routine that includes time for personal study. You can use books, podcasts, or even Youtube motivational videos. Make sure to take notes. Create a consistent routine that nourishes your mind, even if it is only for ten minutes a day.

STEP 5: Learn how to acquire new skills that will give you more choices in life. Skills are massively important in helping you achieve a fulfilling life. The more skills you master, the greater capacity you have to create and sustain a life of wholeness. Skill requires training and conditioning. Remember, the formula is Information + Formation. You can't just read about it.

As part of The Woman School, I created the Skill School program, which gives women formulas to learn foundational skills that we are not taught in our educational system. If you are interested, you can go to thewomanschool.com for more information about the Skill School program.

STEP 6: Find new friends who are investing in their own growth. You are the average of the five people you surround yourself with. So stay vigilant that the people you choose to be in your inner circle are people who understand the value of intentionally designing a fulfilling life. If you don't have those kinds of friends, do not panic, they are out there! You just need to know what you should look for. Use your RAS to help you find them.

STEP 7: Go through this book again and work through the worksheets. It is not a race, you need to work through them and not just get through them. It is not about perfection, it is about progress and taking action. If you don't have the answer, keep going, clarity comes with action. These worksheets have been strategically designed to help you see with eyes of wholeness and integration, to train you to honor every part of yourself. The concepts in this book will not bear fruit in your life unless you take action. The ball is in your court.

If you are interested in additional training, mentorship, accountability, support, and guidance go to thewomanschool.com. We have many options available for you.

Use the following "Dream and Design" worksheet to jumpstart your process and get your wheels spinning about what is possible.

Figure 7.1

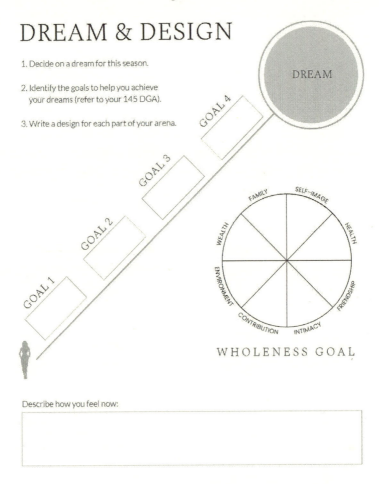

Go to redefinesuccessforwomen.com for a free printable download.

Remember that learning something new is a process. It will take time to learn the new language that you are learning in this book. It will take time to allow these concepts to run through your veins.

It is like remodeling your kitchen. It gets messy before it gets better.

When you are reorganizing your life and transitioning to the life you want, you have to take things apart and figure out what you want and what you don't want.

When women first learn to see with eyes of wholeness, it can feel overwhelming and it is hard to know where to begin, but that is all normal.

Part of remodeling is purging and that is what you are doing through this process. You are getting rid of the old to make room for the new you.

You have to take action.
You have to have someone hold you accountable to take action.
The hardest part is staying the course while seeing only micro progress.

Are you familiar with the growth of the Chinese bamboo tree? You have to water and nurture it for five years every day, and during that time there is little to no visible sign of growth. For five years, there is essentially no change appearing to be taking place. Then suddenly, within the span of five weeks, the tree grows over ninety feet tall! All the actions of watering and nurturing the tree pay off!

I am not saying it will take you five years. What I am saying is that you have to be willing to keep taking action even when you don't receive immediate gratification.

You are going to run into discouragement—that is all part of maturity.

Your ability to choose your highest good is a skill. It is a muscle that needs to be developed.

It will feel like having to gather broken pieces, but I promise you, if you stay the course, it will all make sense. It will eventually look and feel how you want it to be, not perfect but fulfilling. It will be worth your fight.

Be patient and persistent with your progress. This is a lifestyle shift. This is your blueprint for designing a fulfilling life. And, it is just the beginning.

I want to remind you that the destination ought to be as rewarding as the journey.

Your script is, "Progress over perfection."

We use scripts in The Woman School to develop a strong mindset. To access an abundance of scripts, join The Woman School Masterclass, our signature program where we train women how to dream, design their life, and develop themselves.

Below is a worksheet you can use as a guide to using scripts.

Figure 7.2

WHAT I USE SCRIPTS FOR

Go to redefinesuccessforwomen.com for a free printable download.

Remember to be kind to yourself. The kinder you are to yourself, the more you are able to extend that level of kindness to other people.

Redefine Success For You

- Did this book shift your perspective about successful women?
- After reading the content here, how would you describe your own success story?
- How would you define success now, after reading this book?
- How do you feel about shifting the focus of success from achievement to fulfillment?
- Do you want to live a fulfilling life?

Let's review the new definition of success that is rooted in fulfillment.

Success is achieving fulfillment while growing in harmony with your irreplaceable purpose in every season of your life.

To be fulfilled, we need the trifecta of the Fulfillment Formula.

#1: DREAM: We need a *dream*, a vision to aspire to.
#2: DESIGN: We need to *design* a life of wholeness.
#3: DEVELOP: We need to personally *develop* ourselves in order to achieve both our dream and the wholeness design we want for our life.

A woman without a vision will walk aimlessly to a life of exhaustion.

A woman who is not intentionally designing a life of wholeness is at risk of depletion.

Wholeness is about protecting your own fulfillment because you cannot keep giving from an empty cup. It will rob you of your own life.

Wholeness is about having your cup full, so you can pour into other people's cups.

Wholeness is about taking responsibility for your own nourishment so you can nourish the hearts around you.

Wholeness is about living life by design and not by default. It is not an arrival, but rather a constant movement toward your original design, your higher purpose.

Wholeness is a lifestyle of being intentional about how you design every part of your arena.

Wholeness is about taking responsibility for every part of your life and holding yourself accountable to a higher standard so you do not settle into becoming someone you do not want to be.

Wholeness is a way of being that gives you a greater capacity to maximize your full potential so you don't waste your talent or your time on earth.

Wholeness is about designing a life of receptivity for the sake of sustainable generosity.

Wholeness is about making your life an act of generosity.

Wholeness is the path to your fulfillment.

You cannot achieve both the dreams you aspire to and the wholeness design that you want unless you are willing to personally develop yourself.

Your fulfillment requires you to continually develop the woman you need to become in order to achieve the life you want.

Fulfillment requires constant growth.

Fulfillment requires you to expand your mindset and acquire new skills in order to achieve new heights.

Fulfillment requires you to pay attention to your life so you don't miss out on your own life.

Fulfillment requires you to study yourself and be willing to invest in who you need to become.

Fulfillment requires humility. Without humility, this will be impossible. With humility, great things are possible.

The ball of fulfillment is in your court.
You get to decide what you want your life to be.
You get to decide on how you want to write or rewrite your story.

You get to decide on what you need to do right now to begin your own journey to fulfillment.

You can live a meaningful and fulfilling life if you want to.

It is ultimately your choice.

Take note, this choice has serious consequences, not just for you, but also for the people you love.

An unfulfilled woman can become toxic to the people she loves.
An unfulfilled woman can become toxic to her community.
An unfulfilled woman can become toxic to herself.

How you live your life impacts how other people live their lives.

What you choose can create a generational impact on your family.

You hold the keys to your fulfillment.

The Fulfillment Formula I have outlined here for you (page xi) is a proven blueprint to design a fulfilling life. It is used by thousands of people across forty countries and it is creating miracles in their lives. This formula is a blueprint that you can use over and over again to design every season of your life. You are no longer stuck in the life you don't want. At any moment, you can pick up this blueprint and begin the journey to fulfillment again.

Fulfillment is yours for the taking.

Fulfillment is not only attainable, you were created for it.

Fulfillment is what your heart longs for.

Success that is void of fulfillment is unsustainable.

This is why we need to redefine success as rooted in fulfillment, so women no longer have a need to prove their value in the world.

This new definition of success makes success attainable and sustainable for all women.

This new definition includes YOU in whatever season of life you are in. It includes your daughter, your mother, grandmother, sister, friend, co-worker, boss, and all the women in your community who have doubted their unique purpose.

This new definition of success is inclusive.

This new definition of success will raise the standard of how women ought to be treated. It elevates us beyond our achievements.

We all deserve a shot at success.

The time is ripe for us to *Redefine Success For Women*.

This is your proven blueprint to designing a successful life that is rooted in your fulfillment.

My Hope For You

I want to honor you.
If you have made it this far, you are quite a warrior.

It takes a lot of courage to sift through these pages and face hard questions that you might not want to ask yourself.

I am aware that some of these pages will hit you hard, I am sorry.

I knew it was going to be heavy at times and not exactly an easy read, but I also know what this content can do for you. It can change you forever as it has done for thousands of students in The Woman School.

The concepts of this book are not necessarily hard. As a matter of fact, I think they are quite simple. But, they dig deep into our souls.

They force you to look from within and reflect on who you are right now and who you want to become.

Regardless of how you feel about yourself now, I want you to know that you are not alone and you are definitely not stuck. I am fighting alongside you. I am fighting for you. And I will keep fighting for you.

I am fighting for Miss Rosa.
I am fighting for women who doubt their value in the world.

I am fighting for women who have given up their own fight.
I am fighting for women who are tired of having to keep proving they are enough.
I am fighting for my daughters and I am fighting for myself.

There is hope.
I have hope.
There is always hope until our last breath.
Hope will carry us through this war against our worth.

I am a walking testimony of hope and that there is redemption from our wounds.

I wrote this book to awaken your heart and give you permission to dream about the adventures and dreams that are deep within you, just waiting for your 'yes'.

I hope this book will set your heart free to become who you were created to be.
I hope this book will heal your relationship with our Creator.
I hope this book will breathe life in you again.
I hope this book will make you feel alive again.

I hope you never give up on your own life.

I hope you dream of your own success.

I hope you fight to achieve your own fulfillment.

I hope you design a life that is whole, a life that can bring life to those around you.

I hope you continue to develop into the woman you want to become and never lose sight of your purpose.

I hope you will continually invest in yourself so you can invest in the people you love.

I hope you find someone who will cherish all of you and all your imperfections.

I hope you find friends you can cry and laugh with, who hold you accountable for growing into a whole version of yourself.

I hope you can see things with a grateful heart.
I hope you remain generous and trust that the giver always receives the gift back.
I hope you stay patient with yourself.
I hope you are kind to yourself.

I hope you grow in faith—faith in yourself, faith in people, and faith in God.
I hope you find a place you can call home, a place that inspires you.
I hope you can find your passion and use it to bring greater light to the world.

I hope you will live an abundant life, rich in meaning and time well spent.
I hope you will have a family that will usher you to your dreams while cradling you on the rocky road to getting there.

I hope you hear the voice of God in your soul so you can fulfill the very reason why He created you.

I hope you can conquer your fears and never be a slave to them.

I hope you can sit in the quiet and rest your mind, body, and spirit so you can enjoy the simple beauty that life offers.

I hope you can heal old wounds and not allow them to hold you back from loving or living.

I hope you can rise after a fall and find a way to laugh in spite of it all.
I hope you find unshakable peace and joy in your home and in your heart.

I hope you create something beautiful and meaningful with your life.
I hope you find the interior freedom your heart craves.
I hope you discover the deepest desires of your heart and aspire to achieve them.

I hope you can take risks and find something that excites you.
I hope you can stay humble enough to learn something new every day.

I hope you can take a stand against people who devalue your worth and draw the necessary boundaries.

I hope that you can make bold decisions and not allow fear to cripple you into indecision.

I hope you can find the courage to walk away from people who rob you of your worth.

I hope you can go through the challenges in your life with grit and grace.

I hope you live a life that is fully alive.

I hope you continue the good work that you have begun in this book.

I hope you can find the courage to fight for women by fighting for yourself first.

I hope this book gave you enough evidence of your irreplaceable value in the world.

I hope you don't allow the world to make you feel small.

I hope you become the woman you were created to be so you can set the world on fire with your light.

I hope you take up your armor and *Train-Up* for your life's call.

I hope you stay focused and disciplined.

I hope you don't squander the short time you have on earth.

I hope you look back someday with no regrets because you have indeed lived a life fully alive.

Now is your time.

This is your moment to rise up.

You can change your present moment.

You can change the course of history.

You can change your family for generations to come.

You can change the world, beginning with your interior world.

What you offer the world, no one can.

May your life have more life.

May you continue to become a beacon of light for the world.

Keep fighting for your success.

Never, never give up on designing a fulfilling life.
I believe that you can achieve success that fulfills you.

I am fighting for you!

I believe in you.

But even more...

I BELIEVE IN US!

I BELIEVE IN WOMEN.

Let us dare to change the world beginning with our interior world.

Chapter 7

1. Have you compromised your value?
2. How has comparison negatively impacted your life?
3. How are you planning on investing in your fulfillment?
4. Go to thewomanschool.com to join The Woman School army.

EPILOGUE

A CALL TO RISE TOGETHER

You are not here by chance.

You are here by divine providence to play an irreplaceable role in winning the battle for women's worth.

We each have to do our part to bring hope that fulfillment is not only possible for women, but that we were made for it.

We have a duty to share this mission with every facet of society.
We have a duty to share with ALL women a proven path for their own fulfillment.
We have a duty to do our part to heal the brokenness that has allowed women to forget who we are.
We have a duty not just to empower women but to equip them with the practical tools to make their impossible dreams possible.

We have a duty to rebuild culture one 'whole' woman at a time.
We have a duty to fight for our freedom.

It is a privileged time to be a woman.
I believe that we are made for such a time in history.

This is bigger than you, and this is bigger than me.

This is about casting a vision of a future where women are fully alive.

This is our call to rise up.

It is time for courage.

This is our moment to unite against a common enemy that has kept us small and afraid.

This is about raising an army of women who are going to fight for generations to come.

This is about a generational movement to heal from the past, rewrite the present, and embolden the future of all women.

This is our calling and we have the opportunity and honor to change the trajectory for all women now and in the future.

The grace is sufficient for this call.

Together we shall ALL rise.

We won't back down.

I WON'T BACK DOWN!

This is a revolution for our interior freedom—a freedom all women deserve.

Together, we can fight for the freedom to be fully alive.

Let us dare to change the world beginning with our interior world.

It is my honor to fight right alongside you.

Let us go forth and conquer and make this world whole.

A whole world of women FULLY ALIVE!

As Saint Irenaeus tells us, "The glory of God is man fully alive."

I say, *The glory of God is woman fully alive.*

JOIN THE CALL.

LEARN HOW YOU CAN JOIN

THE WOMAN SCHOOL MASTERCLASS

thewomanschool.com

Share this mission

WHAT STUDENTS FROM THE WOMAN SCHOOL ARE SAYING...

January's genius is to take complex ideas and craft them into simple formulas and frameworks that women can easily apply to digestible action steps. –Angela

"I learned more in six months through The Woman School Masterclass than my 4-year college degree. Every woman needs this." –Lisa

"I now have a vision and direction. I now have a strategy to go after the dreams I want. I know my purpose. I have peace. I have a marriage that looks to the future with excitement. I wake up every day excited to keep working toward the woman I want to become. The Woman School Masterclass literally breathed life back into me, my marriage, and my family." –Emily

"I have worked for over ten years as a psychologist in clinical practice. My experience with The Woman School has been nothing short of amazing...as a new Strategist, I am confident that this program will allow me to empower women in a far more efficient, effective, and complete manner than I could in weekly therapy sessions. It is a way to build every aspect of the woman rather than focusing specifically on the challenges they are facing. Women will be surrounded by peers on the journey who are also able to build them up without the stigma associated with diagnoses and a pathology-based approach." –Eve

"Having worked in the healthcare field for over twenty-one years, last year was one of the toughest periods in my life. Navigating the difficulties that came with the pandemic, both personally and professionally, I was at a point in my life where something needed to change. While going through The Woman School Masterclass, I was able to redefine my goals and dreams in all aspects of my life. The Masterclass helped me to manage my mindset during times of extreme stress and overwhelm and at the same time, also helped to improve my relationships with my family, as well as elevate the skills of how I served my patients. I am so honored to now be able to walk with women through this life-changing program..." –Jen

"Until I listened to The Woman School Masterclass, I had no idea that it was my own self-image that needed work. The lessons have taught me how to set boundaries, and how to have difficult conversations with loved ones and others. I did not know that I forgot how to dream. Now, I have tools to recapture some of those dreams, but most importantly, I have become a role model and someone that my friends turn to for sound advice. –Betsy

The Woman School has made such a dramatic, lasting, and positive impact on my life as a mother, wife, daughter, and friend. So much so, that my husband and I now refer to time as either, "before January" or "after January." –Melissa

"The Woman School Masterclass taught me how to be the mother I had always wanted to be, but just couldn't quite figure out before. It taught me intentionality and how to have a peaceful mindset amidst motherhood and busy days. It gave me the freedom to be more myself than ever before!" –Kari

"This is the best investment you can make for yourself and your family. It's a complete 360 for your life." –Haydee

"Recently I have been affirmed on multiple occasions by my therapist that I am not the same person I used to be. I took a two-year hiatus from counseling and during that time I took the Masterclass. She told me to keep doing what I'm doing and is now referring the class to her other clients. THAT means something!" –Karla

"I just finished The Woman School and attended with my daughters. Definitely one of the best decisions we've ever made, we will be using these life lessons forever and will pass them on for generations." –Stephanie

"I've been transformed by this program! The Woman School has given me the tools to dream bigger than I've ever done before. The skills and mindset training have catapulted me to becoming an elevated version of myself and I have the freedom to be able to effectively design the woman, wife, mother, and worker that I want to be as I elevate my own self-image." –Lucy

"The best investment I could make to prepare for post-grad life! So much clarity on who I am and what I want from life that I felt was otherwise missing from my college experience!" –Kate

"I knew within the first few weeks of the program that the Masterclass was more than a quick-fix program, it was a lifestyle. This program has helped me organize my life into different arenas which allows me the ability to be more aware and in control of my beautifully unique life. It has helped me clarify what I want and what I don't want in each aspect of life by unearthing my God-given desires that I have never brought to light before now...It is truly incredible how much I have learned about how bettering myself and my life is actually increasing my ability to be abundantly generous. I recommend this class to all the women in my life who take the time to listen. I find it hard to not talk about The Woman School, especially with women I love and desire the absolute best for. I am so grateful to be a part of this honorable, life-giving program and to be learning alongside these beautiful, inspiring women. The Woman School is a gift from God." –Amber

"My life has been transformed by the Masterclass. One of the greatest privileges that I have experienced is accompanying numerous women on this same journey. I, at one point, was stuck. And as I have worked with women over this past year, I have seen so many women who were stuck regain their spark, regain their hope, and reawaken their dreams." –Angela

"It's difficult to put into words all the ways that The Woman School has helped me. When I first signed up, I didn't even think I needed the course. Most areas of my life were good. I was happy. My husband and children were happy. I thought this was life! But, WOW! After just the first class, I quickly realized that I was spending most of my time letting life happen TO me and not FOR me." –Mary

"Six months ago, my husband noticed that I was cranky, unhappy, and anxious. Six months later after taking the course, he said he noticed a remarkable change that I'm happier, more confident, and becoming more 'me.' He said before, I was merely surviving. After six months, I am now thriving! –Sheila

"My first thought of The Woman School? Fluff, bogus, pyramid scheme, and scam. But after watching my wife work her way through the course it is none of those things. What The Woman School gave her was beyond what I imagined. She became confident in her identity, choices, and purpose. She grew in her faith. She learned how to love herself better and in turn love those around her better. Her days became more structured and more purposeful. She was wonderful then but watching this growth and internal expansion has made me all the more attracted to her. I didn't think it was possible but my wife (who was amazing when I met her) is more amazing now! The Woman School has helped her grow, helped me grow from her growth, and helped our relationship grow from both of us growing! I can't wait to continue to pursue our dream lives together!" –David

"My husband has told me since my TWS journey he feels he's now constantly learning a new version of me. He's been caught off guard by my new reactions to things as opposed to my old defensive ways (obviously, still working on it). But that definitely made me proud of the work I've been putting in thanks to TWS. It creates stronger intimacy on all levels." –Laura

"I spent the past twenty-four years raising kids and now they've been leaving the nest. I thought, "What now?" The Art of Being a Woman Masterclass had me immediately pursuing dreams I thought were dead or meant for the distant future…I have gone from negative thinking and complaining to an attitude of gratitude based on skills I learned through the course. This course has had an impact on my three daughters as well, as I have had the wisdom from The Woman School to coach them through difficult life moments." –Rosanne

"Before The Woman School, I was stuck and searching, wondering if there was more to life. I didn't like the woman I was. So I became a student of The Woman School and over the course of six months, with work and putting in the time, I started to see progress. I learned the skills I needed to manage my thoughts, process my emotions, and create a beautiful life." –Marianna

"The Woman School Masterclass has allowed me to see myself as someone who is visible, someone who has the ability to contribute, and make an impact for the better. I am beautiful and constantly practicing humility and understanding. I am different and unique because there is only one me." –Pauline

"The Woman School Masterclass has given me the tools necessary to combat the negative mindset I have been dealing with for the majority of my life. It has provided me with hope that with skills and scripts, I can have interior freedom and break the generational chain of a negative mindset." –Nicol

"The Woman School Masterclass allowed me to take time to observe where I saw myself trying to please and perform in order to feel appreciated. This was ground-breaking for me in my marriage. There has been a lot of healing through this course, and I was able to see that my self-worth does not rest in the state of my home. It brought such peace to be able to connect with my husband in a new and beautiful way." –Catherine

"The Woman School Masterclass has blessed me with overflowing abundance. I am able to honor my vocation as a wife and mother. I have the tools I need to create a routine, manage my mind, and strategically build the life of my dreams. I am more intentional about my contribution because I am living from a place of integration. The class has transformed all the arenas of my life." –Lauren

"The Woman School Masterclass has helped me overcome so many of my obstacles that were holding me back from becoming the best version of myself. The Woman School has helped me rewire my thoughts and know that my worth is not wrapped up in how big my house is or how much I weigh." –Emmy

"The Woman School has truly been an eye-opening experience for me. I'm so glad I made the choice to invest in myself...I would recommend this class to every single woman!" –Ashley

"The Woman School has given me an awareness of my thoughts and how they impact my life. The Art of Being a Woman Masterclass taught me that my worth is not defined by my accomplishments or failings. It gave me the scripts to replace these negative thoughts and change my mindset so that I can learn the skills to become a whole woman." –Kim

"The Woman School was the best investment in myself. As women, we sometimes don't take care of ourselves first. This class taught me what the fuller version of me looks like. It gave me the skills to better myself in every arena of life so that I can live it by design, not by default!" –Lauren

"The Woman School is a well-constructed journey of transformation. It is rich and enlightening and the content alone is worth the price you pay for the program. But the real jewel of the experience was in the other women who accompanied me, and in Mary, our wise and loving leader (Strategist). I truly felt like I gained sisters and cheerleaders as we all embraced our growth and made it our own." –Holly

"January is doing such important work for women and especially our world! I love how she brings such calm and joy to her work. I really look up to her as a wife and mother and she has really challenged me and helped me grow in my own life." –Nicole

"I can already see a transformation happening in my home, my marriage, my parenting, and friendships as I strive to 'Intentionally work on being a better woman by intentionally elevating each moment toward the highest good!' January is teaching us the skills!" –Elise

"The Woman School Masterclass has changed my mindset completely, giving me the confidence to share my message and my journey, no matter how flawed and full of mistakes..." –Emily

"January has challenged me to continually strive to be a better woman. The issues and truth she discusses touch me to my core. It has been invaluable to realize that I am not alone in my daily struggles and crosses as a woman, wife, and mother. I believe January's witness and message can reach all women wherever they are in their journey." –Becky

"The information and inspiration that The Woman School has provided would cost hundreds of dollars in counseling fees and major time/travel to those sessions. I wish I'd had these courses as a younger woman and young mother, but I can begin anywhere along the path. Thank you for gifting us with this knowledge and practical life skills." –Marcia

LEARN HOW YOU CAN JOIN

THE WOMAN SCHOOL MASTERCLASS

thewomanschool.com

Share this mission

REDEFINE SUCCESS FOR WOMEN

LEARN MORE ABOUT OUR SCHOOLS

WWW.THEWHOLENESSSCHOOL.COM

THEWOMANSCHOOL.COM

THEWHOLENESSSCHOOL.COM

THEWHOLENESSCOACHINGSCHOOL.COM

THEWHOLENESSSCHOOL.COM

Made in the USA
Middletown, DE
22 February 2025

71514857R00206